AMERICAN
GRAPHIC ARTS

To Harry from
Dale Roylance

AMERICAN GRAPHIC ARTS

A Chronology to 1900 in Books, Prints, and Drawings

DALE ROYLANCE

Princeton University Library
PRINCETON, NEW JERSEY
1990

Preface

THIS is an auspicious year for the Graphic Arts Collection, as it marks the fiftieth anniversary of the founding of the collection by Elmer Adler in 1940, as well as the tenth year in the tenure of Dale Roylance as its curator. In a series of exhibitions and publications over the years, Mr. Roylance has called attention to the marvelous group of research materials assembled by Mr. Adler and his successors. This beautifully produced catalogue, *American Graphic Arts: A Chronology to 1900 in Books, Prints, and Drawings*, should be seen both as an extension of that effort and as a companion volume to the earlier catalogue, *European Graphic Arts: The Art of the Book from Gutenberg to Picasso* (Princeton: Princeton University Library, 1986).

In publishing this catalogue, the Library not only calls attention to the resources available in American graphic arts for teaching and research in a variety of scholarly disciplines, but also celebrates the generosity of many donors and collectors who have been central to the development of these holdings. Chief among these is Sinclair Hamilton, Class of 1906, whose collection of "American Illustrated Books to 1870" is among the best to be found anywhere and forms a central component of this exhibition and catalogue. Others whose books and prints are important to the success of this effort include Cyrus H. McCormick, Class of 1879, Grenville Kane, Junius Spencer Morgan, Class of 1888, Moses Taylor Pyne, Class of 1877, Andre deCoppet, Class of 1915, and William Prickett, Class of 1947, among many others. As in so many other recent projects of this nature, moreover, the resources of the Scheide Library have proven to be especially important, and we are grateful to William H. Scheide, Class of 1936, for his continuing cooperation and friendship.

Finally, we extend our warmest thanks to Leonard L. Milberg, Class of 1953, for the many fine books, prints, and drawings he has given to the Library and lent for this exhibition, and for his sustaining interest in the collection and support for our efforts to publicize these holdings. His enthusiastic endorsement of our work has been a source of particular pleasure, and we are especially pleased to acknowledge it.

WILLIAM L. JOYCE
Associate University Librarian for
Rare Books and Special Collections
Princeton, New Jersey
27 December 1989

Acknowledgements

NO ENTERPRISE is possible without the aid of good colleagues. Many of the curators of Rare Books and Special Collections at the Princeton University Library have lent materials in their care to this exhibition and catalogue, and I thank them here. The Scheide Library, with its holdings of extremely rare early American imprints, was made accessible through the kindness of William Scheide and his librarian, William Stoneman. Stephen Ferguson, curator of Rare Books, has also opened the shelves of the Grenville Kane and Cyrus McCormick Collections to supplement the Scheide holdings with some of the earliest and rarest Americana at Princeton. Later periods are chronologically rich due to the combined holdings of the Hamilton, Graphic Arts, Scribner, Adler, and Western Americana collections at Princeton. I thank Alexander Wainwright for several excellent suggestions for early books I had missed. I wish to thank also two Friends of the Princeton University Library, Jean Horblitt and Paul Ingersoll, for their personal loans to the exhibition, colleague Alfred Bush for the loan of his Bierstadt chromolithograph, and the Art Museum for its loan of the Asher Durand and Thomas Eakins prints.

Although this exhibition and catalogue ends at 1900, its production has involved the latest state of computer and printing art in the late twentieth century. For their patient, long hours at the computer keyboard, I am grateful to my assistant in Graphic Arts, Agnes Sherman (St. Agnes), and to my editor Patricia Marks. Proofreading by Patricia Marks, Richard Ludwig, and Joseph Felcone has been invaluable. I owe a particular debt of gratitude to William Joyce for his preface (and steady support in this effort) and to Sinclair Hitchings for his perceptive introduction. The printing and design of the catalogue are the final stage of production, and for this we have the perfectionist work of long-established friends at the Meriden-Stinehour Press.

The original inspiration and help for this exhibition and catalogue came from Leonard L. Milberg, Class of 1953. His many gifts over the past decade may be seen displayed throughout the new wing of Firestone Library. The Leonard L. Milberg Gallery for the Graphic Arts has become an integral part of the Princeton cultural scene. From its first show, "European Graphic Arts: The Art of the Book from Gutenberg to Picasso," in 1983 to the latest display in 1989 of Mrs. Paul Mellon's botanical books and prints, "An Oak Spring Garland," the gallery has attracted a large public. More than all this, Leonard has proved to be a steadfast and supportive friend of the Graphic Arts Collection at Princeton. For this I am profoundly grateful.

DALE ROYLANCE
Curator, Graphic Arts Collection
Princeton University Library

The vignettes decorating the first page of each part of this catalogue are taken from the following books:

BEGINNINGS Theodore de Bry, ed., *Historia Americae sive Novi Orbis. . . .* (Frankfurt, 1591). The Scheide Library.

EIGHTEENTH CENTURY Calligraphic "knot" from *Der Blutige Schau-Platz. . . .* (Ephrata, Pennsylvania, 1749). Graphic Arts, The Sinclair Hamilton Collection.

NINETEENTH CENTURY Daniel Bowen, *A History of Philadelphia. . . .* (Philadelphia, 1849). Graphic Arts, The Sinclair Hamilton Collection.

Introduction

THE ART AND CRAFT of pictorial history is seldom understood, rarely mastered, and yet to be taught. It requires a skillful weaving-together of pictures and words to present facts and insights which open to us some part of the past. A clearly defined theme, mastery of detail, and command of many sources must be combined with book design informed by special experience, if this approach to history is to succeed.

Since 1939 devoted scholars, in a succession of memorable exhibitions and catalogues, have been teaching themselves, and us, their audience, how pictorial history can tell the story of the colonization of North America and the founding and growth of the United States. The enterprise which launched these efforts was the Metropolitan Museum of Art's *Life in America, A Special Loan Exhibition of Paintings Held during the Period of the New York World's Fair*, April 24 to October 29, 1939 (New York, 1939). William M. Ivins, Jr., acting director of the Museum, headed a team which included Stephen C. Clark, Harry B. Wehle, A. Hyatt Mayor, Hermann W. Williams, and Josephine L. Allen.

Other examples of American pictorial history were *From Colony to Nation, An Exhibition of American Painting, Silver and Architecture from 1650 to the War of 1812* (The Art Institute of Chicago, April 21 through June 19, 1949) and the Corcoran Gallery of Art's *American Processional 1492–1900*, published by the National Capital Sesquicentennial Commission, Washington, D.C., in 1950. In 1951 came Marshall B. Davidson's two-volume *Life in America* (Boston: Houghton Mifflin Company in association with the Metropolitan Museum of Art). There have been numerous later exhibitions and catalogues, most notably during the Bicentennial of American Independence in 1976, which took the example of the original *Life in America*, modified it, elaborated on it, and applied it to a specific period or place or other theme in American history.

Dale Roylance's *American Graphic Arts* represents a further evolution of the form described by Francis Henry Taylor in his foreword to Marshall Davidson's *Life in America*:

> The thirst for knowledge, vivid and detailed, has thus brought about a new type of scholarship which gives authority to pictorial representation as a substitute for masses of printed words. The selection and interpretation of these pictures is a new art and constitutes a visual-literary form as revolutionary in our time as was the novel in the eighteenth century and the short story in the nineteenth.

American Graphic Arts will, I believe, be influential, in part because of the clarity with which it establishes moments and episodes in American history within a strongly defined chronological progression; in part, also, because of the brilliant mingling of icons of American history with images that are less known to us. Many books and pictures in these pages have been hallowed from generation to generation in bibliographies, sale catalogues, and exhibition catalogues. Captain John Smith's *Generall Historie* published in London in 1624, for instance, and the map of New England, engraved by Simon de Passe, which is part of the volume, are of such fundamental importance that they may inspire in the student of American history a sense of awe. They are touchstones. Beside such fundamental works, Dale Roylance gives us the ephemeral and the popular—early bookplates and broadsides, chromolithographs, trade cards—and he makes us realize their significance, sometimes intensely private and personal, sometimes reflecting new technology and mass communication.

The book brings us a most extraordinary cast of characters and the opportunity to see not only people but places on a generous scale, in portraits and views. Fact is here, in pictorial reportage, and myth, in imaginings of the New World. We are always close to the printing press in these pages, and to the explorers, artists, writers, mapmakers, composers, caricaturists, advertisers, and others who needed letterpress, copperplate press, lithographic press, or other means of printing to reach their desired audience. Achievements in color printing receive special attention.

Life in America, *From Colony to Nation*, *American Processional*, and many succeeding publications began as exhibitions in which the works exhibited were borrowed from far and wide. *American Graphic Arts*, in contrast, relies almost entirely on a number of exceptional collections at Princeton University, collections which establish Princeton as one of the indispensable centers for research and study in the field, comparable to the New York Public Library, New-York Historical Society, and Library of Congress. The richness of these collections, as we encounter them here, is staggering. Princeton has nurtured American pictorial history through its collectors, authors, and curators. Hyatt Mayor, Class of 1922, and Marshall Davidson, Class of 1928, stand among our most distinguished practitioners, past and present, of this "visual-literary form." Dale Roylance is making a major contribution in Princeton's great tradition.

SINCLAIR HITCHINGS
Keeper of Prints
Boston Public Library

BEGINNINGS

Woodcut depicting King Ferdinand and the discovery of America, from *Lettera di Amerigo Vespucci delle isole nuovamente trouvate in quattre suoi viaggi.* Florence, 1505–1506. The Scheide Library.

The first and most famous printed picture book of the history of the world is Hartmann Schedel's great *Nuremberg Chronicle*. This extraordinary work, first published in 1493, presents in hundreds of bold woodcuts all of the most important events, people, and places—from God and Creation to the author's own time in fifteenth-century Germany. A few blank pages are left at the end for future developments. Remarkably enough, there appeared in the same year a small pamphlet, Giuliano Dati's *Narrative of Columbus* (Florence, 1493), recording a singularly important "future development" left out of the *Nuremberg Chronicle*: the voyage and discoveries of Columbus in 1492. Dati's poetical version of Columbus' 1493 letter to Luis de Santangel includes on its first page a small woodcut which gives us our earliest picture of America. Early printings of this woodcut, including the one in the Scheide Library's *Lettera di Amerigo Vespucci* of 1505–1506, are among the rarest of imprints. Like so many of the woodcuts in the *Nuremberg Chronicle*, a great deal is shown in a very small picture. Here is King Ferdinand on his throne directing a recognizable if miniature Columbus, three famous ships on a deceptively narrow Atlantic Ocean, and the exotic shores of a New World. The long-haired natives, instead of welcoming the Europeans, seem to be doing their best to escape from the picture.

Theodore de Bry, engraving after Jacques Le Moyne de Morgues of Florida Indians at Ribaut's column, from de Bry's *Florida* (*Brevis narratio eorum quae in Florida Americae provincia Gallis acciderunt. . . .*), vol. 2 of de Bry, ed., *Historia Americae sive Novi Orbis. . . .* Frankfurt, 1591. The Scheide Library.

Following Columbus, several explorers—among them Amerigo Vespucci in 1501, Juan Ponce de León in 1513, and Hernando de Soto in 1541—realized that here was not Cathay as Columbus had thought, but a vast unknown land. By 1562 a Frenchman, Jean Ribaut, established a Huguenot settlement in what is now northeastern Florida, and carved the French coat of arms on a stone column to mark the place. Two years later a second band of Frenchmen arrived, led by René de Laudonnière and including a young watercolor artist named Jacques Le Moyne de Morgues. Le Moyne was able to observe at first hand the Indians and their customs. Among the memorable scenes recorded by this highly skilled artist was one of Florida Indians worshipping Ribaut's stone column, in which he included portraits of Laudonnière and the Indian chief Athore.

The Frenchmen's stay was abruptly ended in 1565 when Spanish soldiers attacked the colony. Le Moyne was among the few to escape alive; he returned to Europe, where he found his way to London and the patronage of Sir Walter Raleigh. In the following years Le Moyne reworked in watercolor the scenes he had witnessed in Florida, and these designs came to the attention of the Flemish artist-entrepreneur Theodore de Bry, who was then deeply involved in creating his monumental publishing venture, the *Voyages*. By 1591 de Bry was able to reproduce by copper engraving forty-three of Le Moyne's original designs, all but one of which would otherwise now be lost. The sole surviving Le Moyne watercolor is the scene at Ribaut's column. Today it is one of the New York Public Library's most important iconographical treasures, in beautiful condition, preserving in manuscript an extraordinary picture of a bizarre but friendly encounter of two worlds.

Engraving of a Weroan, or Chieftain, of Virginia by Theodore de Bry after John White, from Thomas Hariot's *A Briefe and True Report of the New Found Land of Virginia*, vol. 1 of de Bry, ed., *Historia Americae sive Novi Orbis. . . .* Frankfurt, 1590. Rare Books. Gift of Arthur A. Houghton, Jr.

Theodore de Bry must again be recognized here for his finely engraved reproduction of a second important set of eyewitness watercolors, this time recording renewed exploration just twenty-one years after Le Moyne's paintings of Florida. This second series was the work of John White, an Englishman sent by Sir Walter Raleigh to help establish the English colony on Roanoke Island, near the mainland of Virginia, in 1584. Unlike the original work of Le Moyne, John White's many sharply observed drawings are all preserved in the British Library, and comprise a priceless pictorial manuscript record of the first English colony in America. Their importance was recognized almost at once by Theodore de Bry, who reproduced by copper engraving twenty-three of them as an illustrated supplement to the first volume of his *Voyages*. Published in 1590, the work was a triumph of graphic arts. There were early editions in Latin, French, German, and English, and seventeen reprintings between 1590 and 1620.

The engraved plates after John White are startling images not only for their exotic subject matter but also for their highly refined engraving. Although they preserve the earliest visual documentation of America, they set up an aesthetic conflict that persists throughout the early history of American picture making: a difficult-to-dispel overlay of European style on American scenery and subjects.

Theodore de Bry was a master engraver of the late sixteenth century, when copper engraving became imbued with all the stylistic elegance of the late Renaissance and the emerging mannerism of the period. The mirrored image of this warrior-chief even recalls the Renaissance convention often used by the Florentine artist Antonio del Pollaiuolo. De Bry's Indians were much copied and imitated, and it was he who established the romantic European image of the American Indian as an elegant savage, an image that lingered on into the nineteenth century, until photography finally established a far more realistic one.

In 1607 a new English settlement was established at Jamestown, Virginia, and in 1609 the Virginia Company of London sent over a fleet of seven ships. Aboard one of them, the *Sea Adventure*, was William Strachey (1572–1621). Strachey kept a careful record of his voyage, including the shipwreck of the *Sea Adventure* in a hurricane off the Bermudas in 1609. His account of this disaster—and of his survival with the ship's crew for ten months as castaways—may have influenced Shakespeare's *The Tempest*.

Strachey spent a year in Jamestown (1610–1611), where he assembled material for his "Historie of Travell into Virginia Britania," written in 1612. This extraordinary manuscript is one of the great treasures of the Princeton University Library. It is of particular interest because it includes as "extra illustration" John Smith's rare 1612 map of Virginia and a group of twenty-seven de Bry engravings after the drawings of John White. All are carefully hand-colored and provide a rich embellishment to Strachey's manuscript account.

Among the de Bry colored engravings inserted in the Strachey manuscript is a view of the Indian village of Secota at Roanoke. It shows in birdseye perspective several houses, gardens growing such eminently American crops as tobacco and corn, as well as pumpkins and sun flowers. In the foreground, Indian customs are included, showing the king's tomb, a feast fire, a feast and a ceremonial dance. The scene conveys a sense of peace and prosperity, confirming Thomas Hariot's optimistic text asserting that "these people live happily together without envy or greed."

Hand-colored engraving of the town of Secota at Roanoke, by Theodore de Bry after John White, in William Strachey, "The Historie of Travell into Virginia Britania." London, 1612. Manuscripts. Gift of Cyrus H. McCormick, Class of 1879. ▶

L
F
E
K
G
H
E
D
B
C
A
TB
20

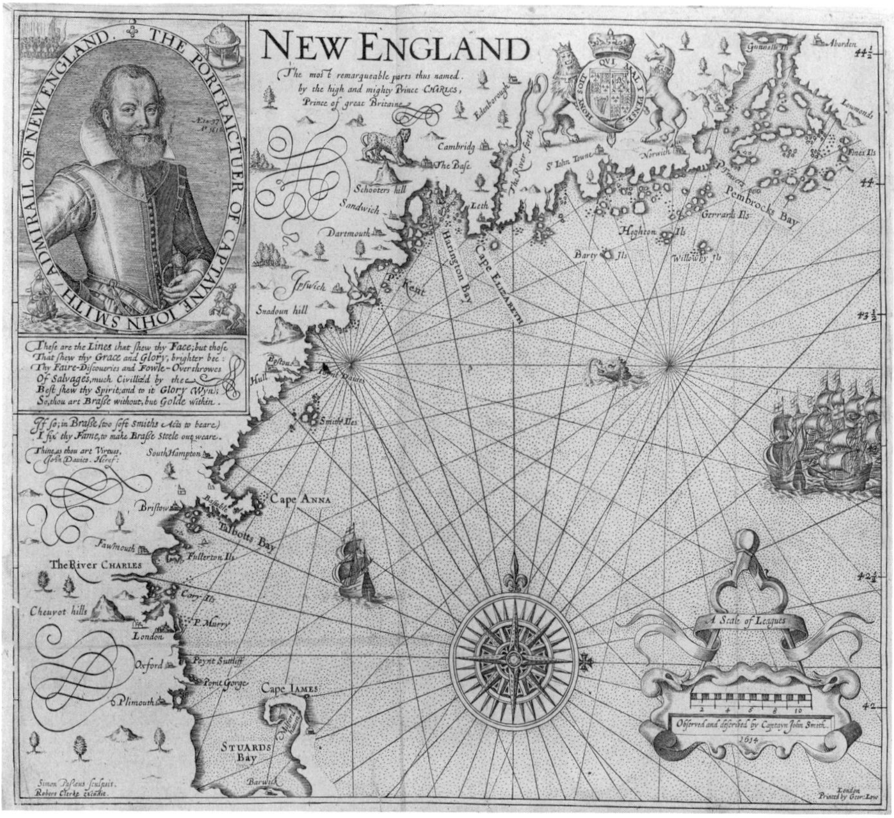

Simon de Passe, engraved map of New England, in John Smith, *The Generall Historie of Virginia, New-England, and the Summer Isles. . . .* London, 1624. Rare Books, The Grenville Kane Collection.

· 1624 ·

The exploration of the northeast coast of North America followed the Jamestown settlement by only a few years. Captain John Smith (1580–1631), who arrived in Jamestown in 1607, spent two years exploring the Chesapeake Bay. Smith continued his relentless travels, and by 1614 had explored and named the northeastern coast "New England." His engraved map fixes in print the English nomenclature for places (including Cambridge and Plymouth). By depicting a European compass rose and the royal coat of arms, and by the prominent placement of the discoverer's portrait, Smith's map declares New England the presumed property of the English crown.

Simon de Passe, engraved portrait of Pocahontas, in John Smith, *The Generall Historie of Virginia, New-England, and the Summer Isles. . . .* London, 1624. Rare Books, The Grenville Kane Collection.

After John Smith returned to England he wrote and had printed a number of extraordinary treatises on both Virginia and New England, all of which are invaluable eyewitness records of early English colonization in America. These works are full of surprising personal recollections, including that best-known of stories, John Smith and the Indian maiden, Pocahontas. When Smith was about to be stoned to death by the Indians, the chief's daughter took his head in her arms "and laid her owne upon it to save him from death."

Pocahontas later married John Rolfe and went with him to England to be received at court. She had her portrait painted in the ruffed and trussed European court dress, transformed at least in costume from an Indian maiden into an English aristocrat. According to Ben Jonson, Pocahontas also became fond of London taverns. She died in 1617 in England, far from her American origins, at age twenty-one.

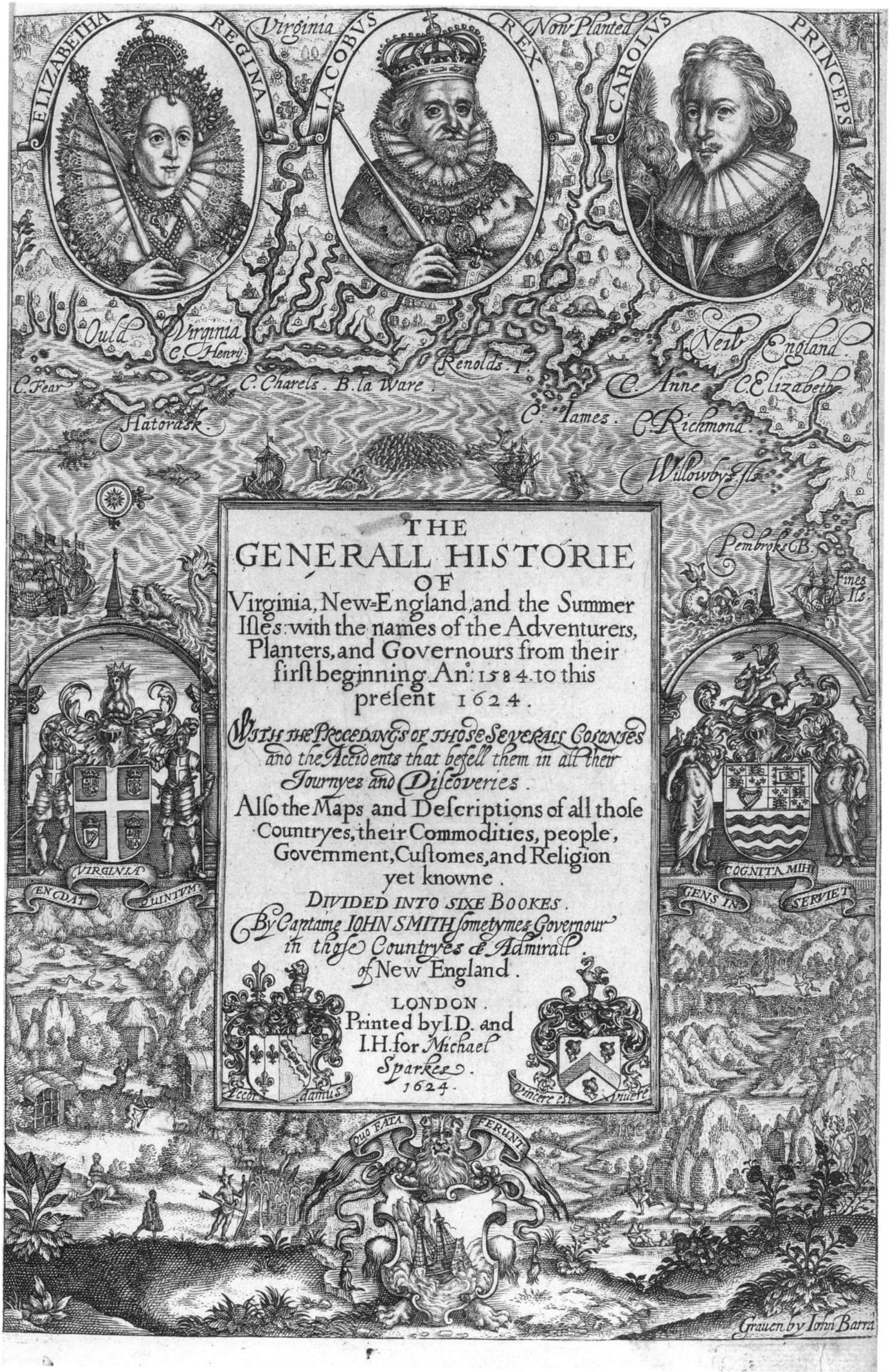

ELIZABETHA REGINA
Virginia
IACOBVS REX
Now Planted
CAROLVS PRINCEPS
Ould Virginia
C. Henry
Renolds I.
C. Fear
C. Charels
B. la Ware
C. Anne
New England
C. Elizabeth
Hatorask
C. James
C. Richmond
Willowbys Ils
Pembroks B.
Fines Ils
THE
GENERALL HISTORIE
OF
Virginia, New-England, and the Summer
Isles: with the names of the Adventurers,
Planters, and Governours from their
first beginning. Ano: 1584. to this
present 1624.
WITH THE PROCEDINGS OF THOSE SEVERALL COLONIES
and the Accidents that befell them in all their
Journyes and Discoveries.
Also the Maps and Descriptions of all those
Countryes, their Commodities, people,
Government, Customes, and Religion
yet knowne.
DIVIDED INTO SIXE BOOKES.
By Captaine IOHN SMITH sometymes Governour
in those Countryes & Admirall
of New England.
LONDON.
Printed by I.D. and
I.H. for Michael
Sparkes.
1624.
VIRGINIA
COGNITA MIHI
QUO FATA FERUNT
Grauen by Iohn Barra

The many editions of John Smith's writings are one of the special strengths of Princeton's Grenville Kane Collection. All are enhanced by his engraved map of New England and by original armorial bindings of the period. John Barn's engraved title page for Smith's *The Generall Historie* is a highly detailed example of much said in little space. The historiated border displays the three successive monarchs of England who ruled over early seventeenth-century North America. In oval miniatures we discover Elizabeth Regina superimposed on her territory of "Ould Virginia," King James I shown on "Virginia now planted" (Raleigh's Virginia of 1607), and King Charles (later editions have *Carolus Rex* with a crown added) on a miniature map of New England. Other engraved details include several tiny scenes based on John White's famous early drawings, and the coats of arms of Virginia and the Bermuda colony ("the Summer Isles"). The wording of the title itself is equally obsessive in its determination to mention every aspect of the abundant information contained in the six sections of this compendium of Smith's several books. Also found in one Princeton copy, which was beautifully bound for Charles I, are complimentary verses by contemporary poets such as John Donne, and the extra-illustration of Pocahontas already described. The book is a complex but wonderful first recapitulation, through European eyes, of early American colonial history.

◀ John Smith, *The Generall Historie of Virginia, New-England, and the Summer Isles. . . .* London, 1624. Rare Books, The Grenville Kane Collection.

THE

VVHOLE
BOOKE OF PSALMES
Faithfully
TRANSLATED *into* ENGLISH
Metre.

Whereunto is prefixed a diſcourſe declaring not only the lawfullnes, but alſo the neceſſity of the heavenly Ordinance of ſinging Scripture Pſalmes in the Churches of God.

Coll. III.

Let the word of God dwell plenteouſly in you, in all wiſdome, teaching and exhorting one another in Pſalmes, Himnes, and ſpirituall Songs, *ſinging to the Lord with grace in your hearts.*

Iames V.

If any be afflicted, let him pray, and if any be merry let him ſing pſalmes.

Imprinted
1640

◂ *The Whole Booke of Psalmes Faithfully Translated into English Metre.* [Cambridge, Massachusetts], 1640; facsimile edition, Chicago, 1956. Graphic Arts.

· 1640 ·

In the summer of 1638, José Glover, a prosperous English Puritan minister, embarked for America with his wife, five children, and servants. Glover, a man of extraordinary vision, took with him a newly purchased printing press and a supply of ink, paper, and foundry types. Glover died in passage, but an enterprising fellow-passenger, a locksmith named Stephen Day (or Daye) and his son Matthew, worked with Glover's widow to establish the first North American printing press at Cambridge, Massachusetts, in 1638. It was less than ten years after the Massachusetts Bay Colony itself had been founded; along with the establishment of the first College Library at Harvard in 1638, the press represented early recognition of intellectual independence in the New World.

According to John Winthrop's manuscript journal, the first printing of the Cambridge press was the *Almanack, Calculated for New England*, followed by the celebrated "Freeman's Oath." No copies of either survive. The third work was far more ambitious: *The Whole Booke of Psalmes Faithfully Translated into English Metre.* Matthew Day produced 1,700 copies of this first book printed in British America. Only eleven copies have survived, making it much more rare than the first European printed book, the Gutenberg Bible. The "Bay Psalm Book" does not share any of the splendid qualities of Gutenberg's work; instead, it reveals Stephen and Matthew Day's lack of training in the printer's craft. This was probably of little concern to the Puritans: "To make life more beautiful was not the motive which led to the settlement of New England. . . . The typography [of the Cambridge Press] was as unattractive and crabbed as the matter which it (perhaps fittingly) enshrined."* Extraordinary strength of purpose, however, and its place as the first book printed in British North America, give the Bay Psalm Book its own great historical importance.

* Daniel Berkeley Updike, *Printing Types*, 2 vols. (Cambridge, Massachusetts, 1922); Vol. 2, pp. 149–150.

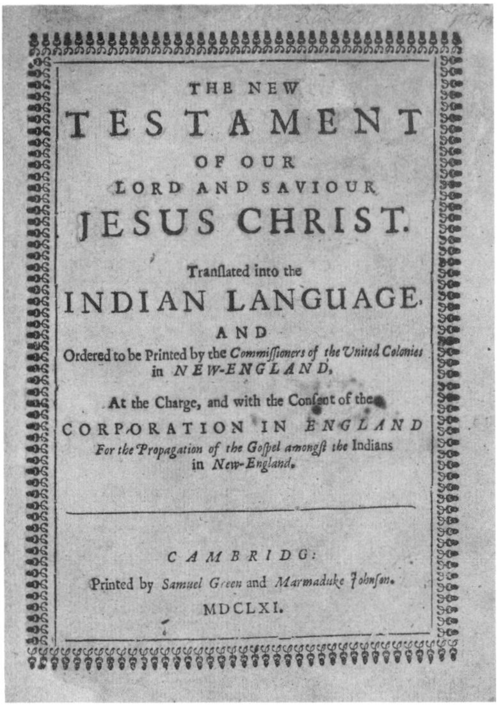
THE NEW
TESTAMENT
OF OUR
LORD AND SAVIOUR
JESUS CHRIST.
Tranflated into the
INDIAN LANGUAGE.
AND
Ordered to be Printed by the Commiffioners of the United Colonies
in NEW-ENGLAND,
At the Charge, and with the Confent of the
CORPORATION IN ENGLAND
For the Propagation of the Gofpel amongft the Indians
in New-England.
CAMBRIDG:
Printed by Samuel Green and Marmaduke Johnfon.
MDCLXI.

John Eliot, translator, *The New Testament . . . Translated into the Indian Language.* . . . Cambridge, 1661. The Scheide Library.

· 1661–1663 ·

The press at Cambridge continued through two decades of religious publication. Its efforts culminated in 1663 with the printing of 1,500 copies of a book known as the "Eliot Indian Bible." This monumental task was undertaken by John Eliot, a Puritan preacher of the Bay Colony, and only extreme missionary zeal could have made him persevere. Eliot, supported by the "Society for the Propagation of the Gospell in New England," finished translating the Bible into the Algonquin language by 1655. Two heroically dedicated printers, Samuel Green and Marmaduke Johnson, were able to complete printing the New Testament in 1661, and the Old Testament in 1663.

The Scheide Library at Princeton is rich in early American imprints, and particularly in the works of John Eliot. It includes Eliot's *Indian Grammar* (1666) and the eleven "Indian Tracts," all of the greatest rarity.

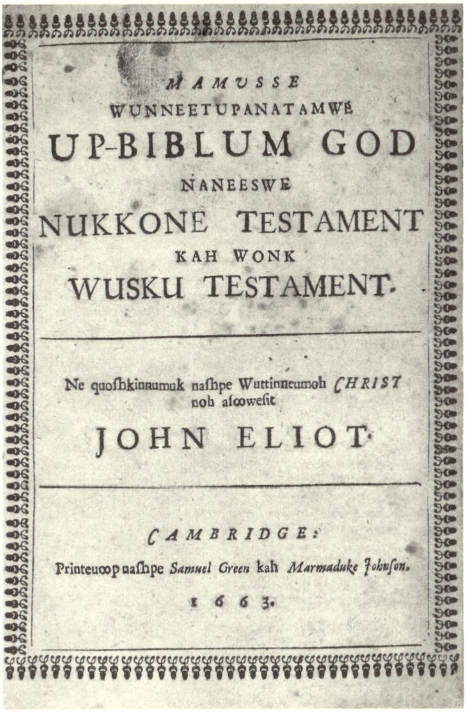
MAMUSSE
WUNNEETUPANATAMWE
UP-BIBLUM GOD
NANEESWE
NUKKONE TESTAMENT
KAH WONK
WUSKU TESTAMENT.

Ne quoshkinnumuk nashpe Wuttinneumoh *CHRIST*
noh asoowesit
JOHN ELIOT.

CAMBRIDGE:
Printeuoop nashpe *Samuel Green* kah *Marmaduke Johnson.*
1663.

John Eliot, translator, *Mamusse wunneetupanatamwe up-Biblum God.* . . . [The Eliot Indian Bible]. Cambridge, 1663. The Scheide Library.

· 1663 ·

Printing a book in a totally strange language was a truly arduous piece of work for two of our earliest printers. Fortunately, John Eliot, after translating the text, did convert at least one Indian not only to the faith, but to the art of printing as well. This Indian youth did much to assist Samuel Green and Marmaduke Johnson in the printing of this first American Bible. He was named James the printer, or James Printer, by his mentor John Eliot, and became our first native-born craftsman. There is a possibility that James Printer tried his hand at binding as well as printing. Among the extraordinary Eliot imprints in the Scheide Library is a crudely bound copy of the second edition of 1685 that may be the binding effort of James Printer himself.*

* Gordon M. Marshall, Jr. "Americana in the Scheide Library," *Princeton University Library Chronicle*, Vol. 37, No. 2 (Winter 1976) 154–168.

John Foster, woodcut portrait, "Mr. Richard Mather." Cambridge, Massachusetts, 1670. Graphic Arts, The Sinclair Hamilton Collection. Gift of the family of Frank Jewett Mather, Jr.

· 1670 ·

The first print made in North America is this portrait, cut in wood by our first American-born printmaker, John Foster. Like so many painters of primitives in early America, Foster presents a three-quarter view of his subject looking at us with an honest confrontational stare. The subject of the woodcut portrait is Richard Mather who, with John Eliot and Thomas Weld, prepared the Bay Psalm Book and wrote its preface. In one hand Mather holds his spectacles, in the other the book which seems to be in size and typography the Bay Psalm Book itself.

While technically crude, the woodcut portrait has a strong graphic effect that evidently pleased the young Foster, for he went on to create in 1677 the first map made in America, again cut in wood, but with far more technical expertise.

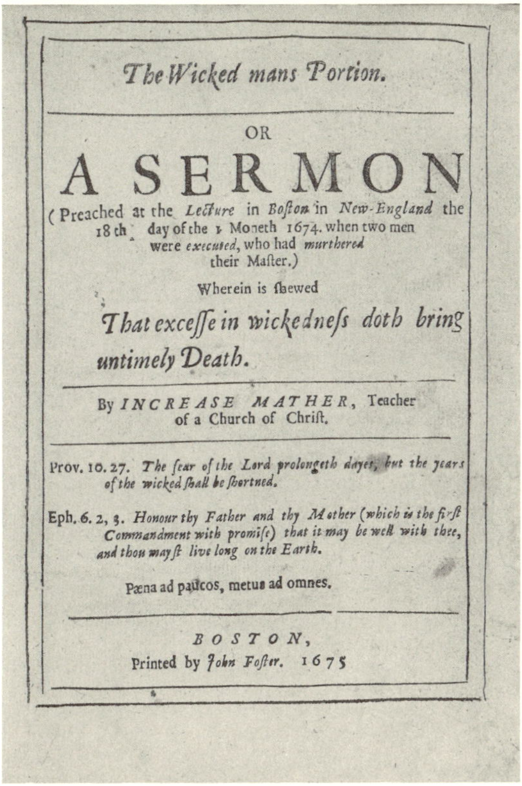

The Wicked mans Portion.

OR

A SERMON

(Preached at the *Lecture* in *Boston* in *New-England* the 18th day of the 1 Moneth 1674. when two men were *executed*, who had *murthered* their Mafter.)

Wherein is fhewed

That exceffe in wickednefs doth bring untimely Death.

By *INCREASE MATHER*, Teacher of a Church of Chrift.

Prov. 10.27. *The fear of the Lord prolongeth dayes, but the years of the wicked fhall be fhortned.*

Eph. 6. 2, 3. *Honour thy Father and thy Mother (which is the firft Commandment with promife) that it may be well with thee, and thou mayft live long on the Earth.*

Pæna ad paucos, metus ad omnes.

BOSTON,
Printed by *John Fofter*. 1675

Increase Mather, *The Wicked Mans Portion. or A Sermon. . . .* Boston, 1675.
The Scheide Library.

· 1675 ·

John Foster must have become increasingly pleased and preoccupied with the possibilities of printing in America. By 1674 he had acquired his own press and typefaces from Marmaduke Johnson in Cambridge, and established himself on the other side of the Charles River to create the first printing office in Boston. The first book he printed was Increase Mather's *The Wicked Mans Portion*, a book full of the dark tone of sin and damnation that haunts so much of the printing of Puritan New England. The Puritan clergy, like their forebears in fifteenth-century Europe, were quick to recognize the power of print for religious conversion, and the incunabula of the first fifty years of printing in British America are dominated by dogmatic religious texts.

Book label dated 1675, in John Cotton's copy of Henrich Smet, *Prosodia.* Frankfurt, 1620. Rare Books.

· 1675 ·

The first president of Harvard College, Henry Dunster, had his small ornament-fringed bookplate printed in England in 1629. Dunster's book label was imitated for other book collections in Cambridge, Massachusetts, as early as 1652. Printed on the same press that had produced the Bay Psalm Book in 1640, it is the earliest known American bookplate.*

In recent years a similar book label of the seventeenth century was discovered in a book in the open stacks of the Princeton University Library. Dated June 5, 1675, this small scrap of paper is a unique dated record of printed ephemera, also perhaps from the Cambridge press, as well as an evocative association copy of John Cotton, a book-collecting classmate of Cotton Mather.**

* Edward Naumburg, Jr., "A Seventeenth-Century Book Label Problem," *The New Colophon*, Vol. 2, Part 5 (January 1949), p. 43.

** M. Halsey Thomas, "An Early American Book Label," *Princeton University Library Chronicle*, Vol. 22, No. 1 (Autumn 1960), 36–37.

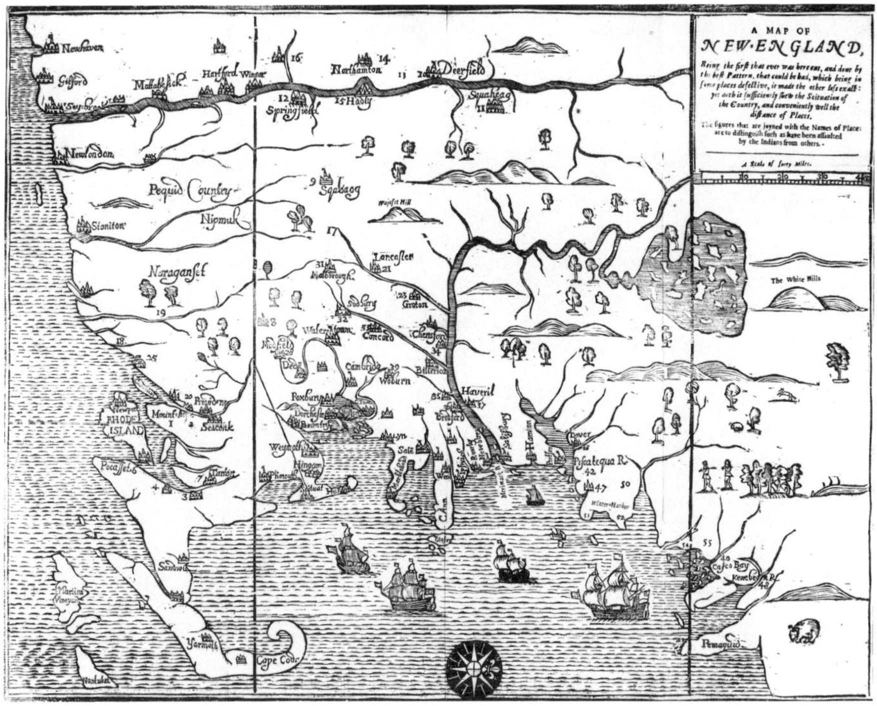

John Foster, woodcut, "Map of New England . . . " (The "White Hills Map"), in William Hubbard, *The Present State of New-England, Being a Narrative of the Troubles with the Indians*. . . . Boston, 1677. Graphic Arts, The Sinclair Hamilton Collection.

· 1677 ·

The second known woodcut by John Foster is more truly intended as a book illustration, and carries the proud printed title "Map of New-England, Being the first that ever was here cut." It was the first map of any kind to be printed in North America, and begins American-made cartography. Since it is a clear-cut elucidation of the text by Hubbard it must also be seen as the beginning of book illustration in our country.

Another version of this rare woodcut map is known as the "Wine Hills Map" because of an error in the London edition of 1677; it is in the Grenville Kane Collection's copy of Hubbard's work, also at Princeton.

Abraham in Arms; or, The First Religious General with His Army Engaging in a War. . . . Boston, 1678. Graphic Arts, The Sinclair Hamilton Collection. *(detail, enlarged)*

· 1678 ·

This woodcut vignette, with its traditional strap-work and trumpet-blowing cherubs, is very much in the style of European baroque book decoration. It may have been imported by John Foster for use in his printing, but James Thomas Flexner, in his *First Flowers of Our Wilderness* (1947), believes it to be Foster's own work, and even describes it as possibly his trademark. The inclusion in the center cameo of a nonchalant skeleton at royal ease on his coffin gives a true New England gravestone touch to the cut.

Broadside, *At a Council held at Boston, March 8, 1679/80.* . . . Boston, 1680. Graphic Arts, The Sinclair Hamilton Collection.

· 1680 ·

More certainly from John Foster's hand is the woodcut used in his printing of official broadsides of Massachusetts. It is also the earliest picture of an Indian printed in America and shows an open-armed, friendly native with bow and arrow, saying on the ribbon that issues from his mouth, "Come over and help."

John Foster, our first American printmaker, mapmaker, and book illustrator, died in 1681, a fact recorded in the *Annals of Dorchester*, where we also learn that John Foster was a "Schoolmaster of Dorchester, and he that made the then Seal or Arms of Ye Colony, namely an Indian with a bow and arrow."

J. van Vienen,, engraving, "Niagara Falls" (the earliest printed picture of Niagara Falls), from Father Louis Hennepin, *A New Discovery of a Vast Country in America*. . . . London, 1698. Rare Books, The Grenville Kane Collection.

· 1698 ·

While the earliest American prints and printing were finding their first primitive expression in New England, exploration and discovery continued into the vast, still unknown continent to the West. The most spectacular of American natural wonders, Niagara Falls, was discovered in 1678 by a French travelling friar, Louis Hennepin, and subsequently described by him in 1697. Truly thrilled, Hennepin wrote of "a vast prodigious Cadence of Water which falls down after a surprising and astonishing manner, insomuch that the Universe does not afford its parallel." Others would be equally enthralled, and Niagara Falls became a form of religious experience for many writers and artists in America of the eighteenth and nineteenth centuries. To Europeans, this vast cataract must have presented overwhelming evidence that America was a terrifying unknown, full of wild scenery, and as far from the gentility of home as anyone could imagine.

EIGHTEENTH CENTURY

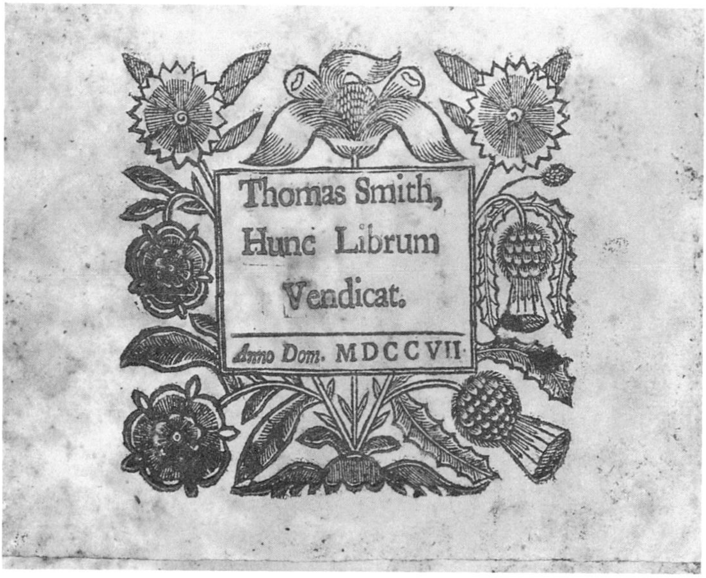

The bookplate of Thomas Smith, 1707, pasted on the inside front cover of Nicolas Bound, *Sabbathum veteris et Novi Testamenti*. London, 1706. Graphic Arts, The Sinclair Hamilton Collection.

· 1707 ·

Described by Sinclair Hamilton as "probably the first ornamental American bookplate," this Thomas Smith *ex libris*, with its woodcut border bouquet of Tudor roses and thistles, is an almost springlike emergence from the dark sobriety of earlier Puritan typography. It is a rare early bloom of a new printers' garden of ornament that would eventually bring European rococo book decoration to American printing.

The FARMERS
ALMANACK
For the Year 1714.

By N. W. A Lover of the Truth.

Long Live Queen ANNE in Peace and Glorious Reign,
The World's Rare Wonder, and our Great Sov'raign.

A R

From Heav'n above on Her Great Blessings flow,
That She may Reign, and on us Favour show.

That She may be true Protestants Great Defender,
And of the True Religion She may be most Tender.

Beneath her Feet let all Her En'mies low'r,
And never rise against Her any more.

America: Printed for the Author: And are to be Sold by N. Boone, at the Sign of the Bible in Boston, 1714.

The Farmer's Almanack for the Year 1714. Boston, 1714. Graphic Arts, The Sinclair Hamilton Collection.

· 1714 ·

The title-page portrait is of Queen Anne, and is the first woodcut to appear in an American eighteenth-century book. Earlier New England primers must have had similar small woodcuts, but none of these has survived. The portrait also appears to be a naive but careful copy in wood of a European copper engraving, including all the *cartouche* border conventions so characteristic of European baroque prints.

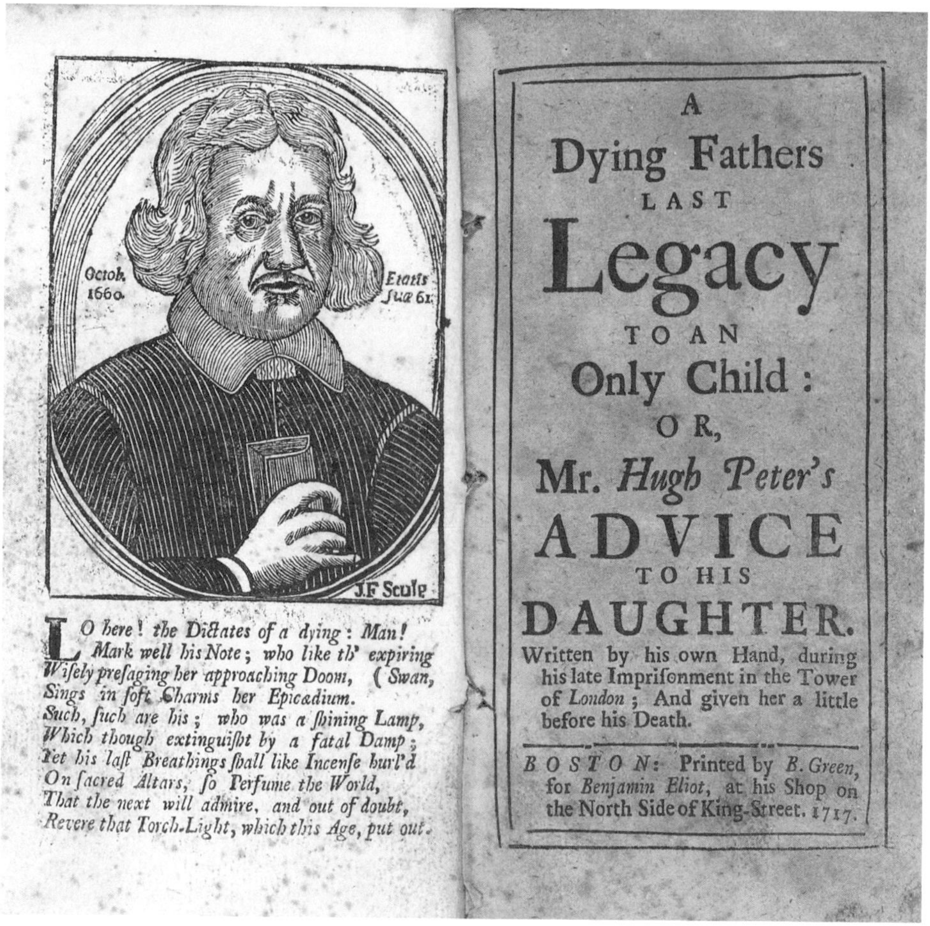

LO here! the Dictates of a dying: Man!
Mark well his Note; who like th' expiring
Wisely presaging her approaching Doom, (Swan,
Sings in soft Charms her Epicedium.
Such, such are his; who was a shining Lamp,
Which though extinguisht by a fatal Damp;
Yet his last Breathings shall like Incense hurl'd
On sacred Altars, so Perfume the World,
That the next will admire, and out of doubt,
Revere that Torch-Light, which this Age, put out.

A
Dying Fathers
LAST
Legacy
TO AN
Only Child:
OR,
Mr. *Hugh Peter's*
ADVICE
TO HIS
DAUGHTER.
Written by his own Hand, during his late Imprisonment in the Tower of *London*; And given her a little before his Death.

BOSTON: Printed by *B. Green*, for *Benjamin Eliot*, at his Shop on the North Side of King-Street. 1717.

A Dying Father's Last Legacy to an Only Child. . . . Boston 1717. Graphic Arts, The Sinclair Hamilton Collection.

· 1717 ·

Woodcut primitives, as they appear in early American illustrated books, offer a lesser-known graphic equivalent of painted portrait primitives. American painting emerged from a school of itinerant, usually self-taught "limners," and the same may be said of early woodcut illustration. This example, while signed "J. F. sculp." in the wood and very much in the tradition of our first primitive John Foster, is probably the work of James Franklin, the elder brother of Benjamin Franklin and an active printer in Boston at this time.

John Bunyan, *Grace Abounding to the Chief of Sinners. . . .* Boston, 1729.
Graphic Arts, The Sinclair Hamilton Collection.

· 1717 ·

Not surprisingly, John Bunyan was a favorite author among Puritan New Englanders. His *Pilgrim's Progress* was printed in America as early as 1681, and remained in print in constant new editions throughout the eighteenth and nineteenth centuries. Princeton's Sinclair Hamilton Collection alone includes illustrated editions of 1729, 1791, 1793, 1794, 1800, 1804, 1805, 1806, 1817, 1818, 1819, 1837, 1846, and 1852, demonstrating this book's seemingly indestructible appeal to an American reading public preoccupied with sin and salvation. The woodcut portrait of Bunyan is thought to have appeared as early as 1717, and may well be the work of James Franklin.*

* David E. Smith, "Illustrations of American Editions of *The Pilgrim's Progress*," *Princeton University Library Chronicle*, Vol. 26, No. 1 (Autumn 1964), 16–26.

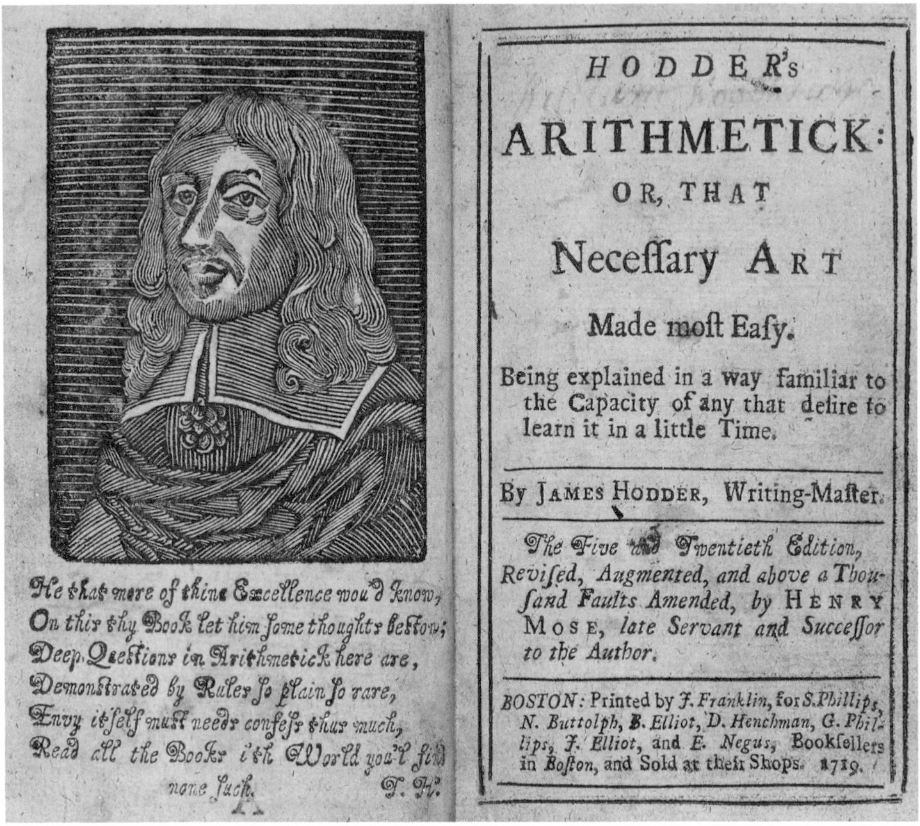
He that more of thine Excellence would know,
On this thy Book let him some thoughts bestow;
Deep Questions in Arithmetick here are,
Demonstrated by Rules so plain so rare,
Envy itſelf must needs confeſs thus much,
Read all the Books i'th World you'l find none such.
J. H.

HODDER's
ARITHMETICK:
OR, THAT
Neceſſary ART
Made moſt Eaſy.
Being explained in a way familiar to the Capacity of any that deſire to learn it in a little Time.

By JAMES HODDER, Writing-Maſter.

The Five and Twentieth Edition, Reviſed, Augmented, and above a Thouſand Faults Amended, by HENRY MOSE, late Servant and Succeſſor to the Author.

BOSTON: Printed by J. Franklin, for S. Phillips, N. Buttolph, B. Elliot, D. Henchman, G. Phillips, J. Elliot, and E. Negus, Bookſellers in Boſton, and Sold at their Shops. 1719.

James Hodder, *Hodder's Arithmetick: or, That Necessary Art Made Most Easy.* Boston, 1719. Graphic Arts, The Sinclair Hamilton Collection.

· 1719 ·

The printer James Franklin may have made the woodcut frontispiece for this first American edition of James Hodder's classic English textbook on arithmetic, first printed in London in 1661. Below the attractively primitive rendering of the author's portrait is a typical set of English rhymes by Hodder, enticing the reader into the book. The lines are set in an ornate typeface known as "swash italic," very unusual for such an early American printing. Since Benjamin Franklin was an apprentice in his older brother's shop at this time, it is tempting to think he may have set the type, and that his later strong interest in such ingenious calligraphic types may have been aroused by his work on this book.

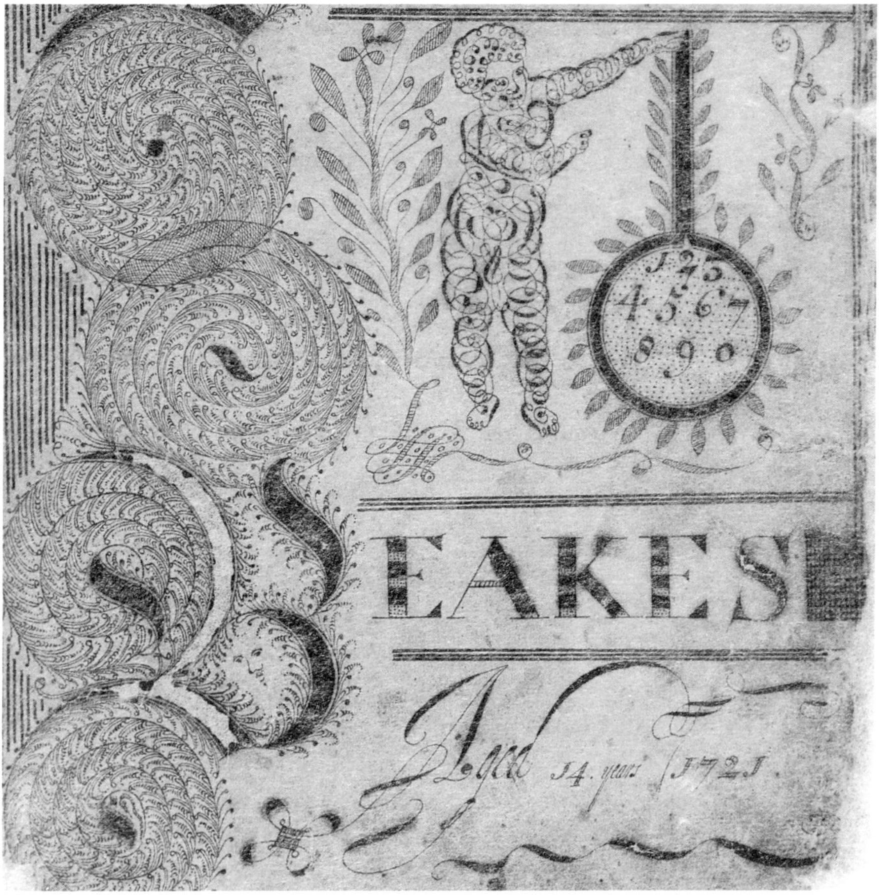

Stacy Beakes, a calligraphic manuscript on mathematics. Trenton, New Jersey, signed and dated 1721. Manuscripts. Gift of Daniel Maggin. (*detail*)

· 1721 ·

This extraordinary mathematical notebook, or "ciphering book," is the work of a fourteen-year-old Trenton, New Jersey, boy named Stacy Beakes. He must have been a child wonder, or had a tutor's extensive help. Where Hodder's *Arithmetick* of 1719 made that art "most easy," young Beakes goes into the most abstruse eighteenth-century mathematics and geometry. In addition, the manuscript is rendered in a well-trained calligraphic hand throughout, and is full of the ornate flourishes characteristic of aristocratic penmanship in England.

Mark Catesby, hand-colored engravings, "The Great Booby" and "Magnolia Altissima . . ." from *The Natural History of Carolina, Florida, and the Bahama Islands*. London, 1731–1748. Rare Books.

· 1731 ·

Catesby's *Natural History of Carolina* is among the first delineations of American plants and animals since the seventeenth-century watercolor studies done by Jacques Le Moyne de Morgues and John White. It was published in London in parts from 1731 to 1743 following Catesby's extensive travels in Virginia and Carolina. After his return to England, Catesby took lessons in drawing and etching, so that he was able to delineate and engrave the 220 plates of his ambitious work himself. Another indication of his tireless devotion to this book is that the first two editions were completely hand-colored by Catesby himself.

John Carwitham, *A View of Fort George with the City of New York from the S. W.* Engraving. London, 1731. Lent by Leonard L. Milberg, Class of 1953.

· 1731 ·

This is a rare early printed view of New York from the New Jersey side of the Hudson River. The landmark steeple of Trinity Church is clearly visible on the left, one of the very few survivors of early New York in present-day Manhattan. The composition seems to be based on an earlier view of Fort George by William Burgis. Both prints have as a prominent foreground feature a proud British man-of-war in full sail with all cannons blasting away. Union Jacks fly on both the ships and above the port, giving a strong British colonial stamp to this early view of New York.

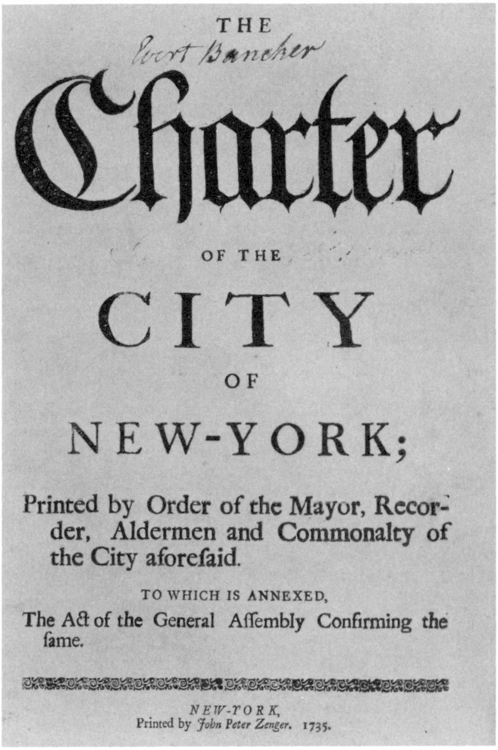
THE

Charter

OF THE

CITY

OF

NEW-YORK;

Printed by Order of the Mayor, Recorder, Aldermen and Commonalty of the City aforesaid.

TO WHICH IS ANNEXED,

The Act of the General Assembly Confirming the same.

NEW-YORK,
Printed by *John Peter Zenger.* 1735.

The Charter of the City of New-York. . . . New York, 1735. Rare Books, The Grenville Kane Collection.

· 1735 ·

John Peter Zenger left Germany at age thirteen to become an apprentice to William Bradford in New York City. In 1733, in his own shop, Zenger founded the *New York Weekly Journal*, which became a highly controversial political newspaper. After its first year of publication, Zenger was arrested on a charge of seditious libel. Attorney Andrew Hamilton brilliantly defended Zenger, and won this historic case for freedom of the press. Gouverneur Morris described the verdict as "the morning star of that liberty which subsequently revolutionized America." Zenger became a highly respected printer, and in 1735 he issued one of his finest works, *The Charter of the City of New-York*, using with Germanic flourish a proud display of 72-point black letter for the word "Charter." The book's careful layout, the letter-spacing, and clear impression, together with this copy's beautiful binding, bespeak unusual concern for typography and design.

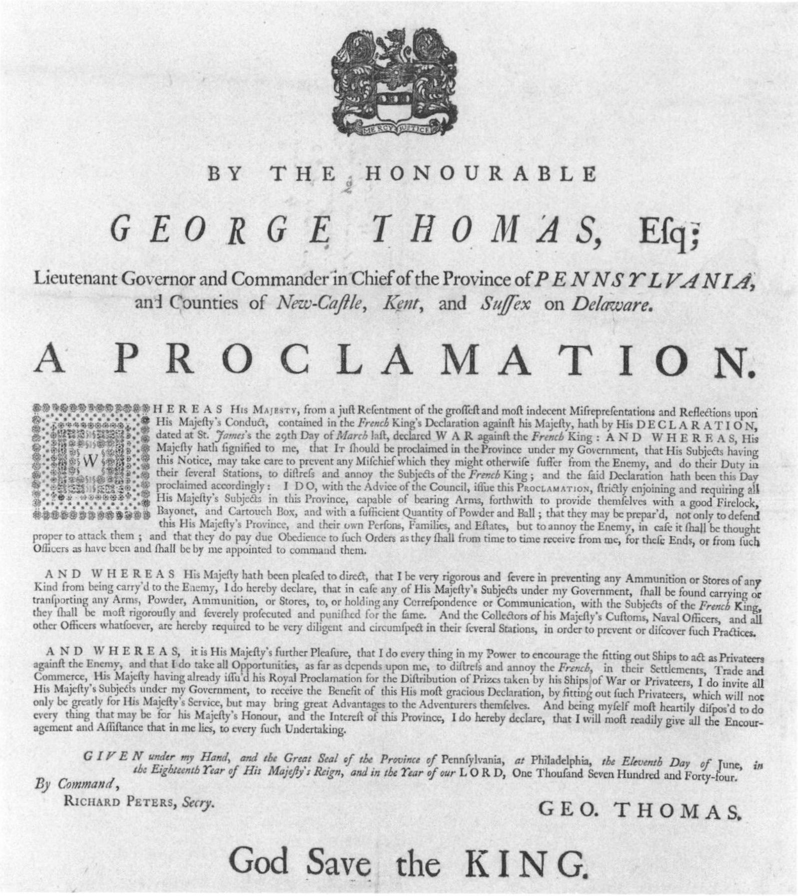

BY THE HONOURABLE

GEORGE THOMAS, Eſq;

Lieutenant Governor and Commander in Chief of the Province of *PENNSYLVANIA*, and Counties of *New-Caſtle*, *Kent*, and *Suſſex* on *Delaware*.

A PROCLAMATION.

WHEREAS His MAJESTY, from a juſt Reſentment of the groſſeſt and moſt indecent Miſrepreſentations and Reflections upon His Majeſty's Conduct, contained in the *French* King's Declaration againſt his Majeſty, hath by His DECLARATION, dated at St. *James*'s the 29th Day of *March* laſt, declared WAR againſt the *French* King: AND WHEREAS, His Majeſty hath ſignified to me, that IT ſhould be proclaimed in the Province under my Government, that His Subjects having this Notice, may take care to prevent any Miſchief which they might otherwiſe ſuffer from the Enemy, and do their Duty in their ſeveral Stations, to diſtreſs and annoy the Subjects of the *French* King; and the ſaid Declaration hath been this Day proclaimed accordingly: I DO, with the Advice of the Council, iſſue this PROCLAMATION, ſtrictly enjoining and requiring all His Majeſty's Subjects in this Province, capable of bearing Arms, forthwith to provide themſelves with a good Firelock, Bayonet, and Cartouch Box, and with a ſufficient Quantity of Powder and Ball; that they may be prepar'd, not only to defend this His Majeſty's Province, and their own Perſons, Families, and Eſtates, but to annoy the Enemy, in caſe it ſhall be thought proper to attack them; and that they do pay due Obedience to ſuch Orders as they ſhall from time to time receive from me, for theſe Ends, or from ſuch Officers as have been and ſhall be by me appointed to command them.

AND WHEREAS His Majeſty hath been pleaſed to direct, that I be very rigorous and ſevere in preventing any Ammunition or Stores of any Kind from being carry'd to the Enemy, I do hereby declare, that in caſe any of His Majeſty's Subjects under my Government, ſhall be found carrying or tranſporting any Arms, Powder, Ammunition, or Stores, to, or holding any Correſpondence or Communication, with the Subjects of the *French* King, they ſhall be moſt rigorouſly and ſeverely proſecuted and puniſhed for the ſame. And the Collectors of his Majeſty's Cuſtoms, Naval Officers, and all other Officers whatſoever, are hereby required to be very diligent and circumſpect in their ſeveral Stations, in order to prevent or diſcover ſuch Practices.

AND WHEREAS, it is His Majeſty's further Pleaſure, that I do every thing in my Power to encourage the fitting out Ships to act as Privateers againſt the Enemy, and that I do take all Opportunities, as far as depends upon me, to diſtreſs and annoy the *French*, in their Settlements, Trade and Commerce, His Majeſty having already iſſu'd his Royal Proclamation for the Diſtribution of Prizes taken by his Ships of War or Privateers, I do invite all His Majeſty's Subjects under my Government, to receive the Benefit of this His moſt gracious Declaration, by fitting out ſuch Privateers, which will not only be greatly for His Majeſty's Service, but may bring great Advantages to the Adventurers themſelves. And being myſelf moſt heartily diſpos'd to do every thing that may be for his Majeſty's Honour, and the Intereſt of this Province, I do hereby declare, that I will moſt readily give all the Encouragement and Aſſiſtance that in me lies, to every ſuch Undertaking.

GIVEN under my Hand, and the Great Seal of the Province of Pennſylvania, *at* Philadelphia, *the Eleventh Day of* June, *in the Eighteenth Year of His Majeſty's Reign, and in the Year of our* LORD, One Thouſand Seven Hundred and Forty-four.

By Command,
RICHARD PETERS, *Secry.*

GEO. THOMAS.

God Save the KING.

Benjamin Franklin, printed broadside, *By the Honourable George Thomas, Esq., Lieutenant Governor and Commander in Chief of the Province of Pennsylvania . . . A Proclamation.* Philadelphia: Benjamin Franklin, 1744. Graphic Arts, The Sinclair Hamilton Collection.

· 1744 ·

This handsome folio broadside is the work of the young Benjamin Franklin, and beautifully displays the sophisticated typography of this most famous and able of colonial American printers. Printed in 1744, the same year as the book recognized as his printing masterpiece, Cicero's *Cato Major* (also at Princeton), this broadside shows the same sensitivity to letter-spacing, use of ornament, and clean letterpress impression as that achieved by his celebrated English contemporaries, Caslon and Baskerville.

Mr. BENJAMIN KEACH.

The Progreſs of *S I N*,

OR THE

Travels of *Ungodlineſs.*

Wherein the *Pedigree*, *Riſe* (or *Original*) *Antiquity*, *Subtilty*, *evil Nature*, and *prevailing Power* of SIN is fully diſcovered; in an apt and pleaſant

ALLEGORY:

Together with the great VICTORIES he hath obtained, and abominable *Evils* he hath done to Mankind by the Help of the *DEVIL*, in all his *Travels*, from the Beginning of the World to this very Day.

As alſo the Manner of his *Apprehenſion*, *Arraignment*, *Trial*, *Condemnation*, and *Execution*.

By *Benjamin Keach*:

Author of the Travels of *True Godlineſs*, *War with the Devil*, and *Sion in Diſtreſs*.

The SIXTH EDITION corrected: *With ſome Additions by the Author.*

BOSTON: Printed by *B. Green* and Comp. for *D. Gookin* at the Corner of *Water-ſtreet*. 1744.

Benjamin Keach, *The Progress of Sin, or The Travels of Ungodliness. . . .* Boston, 1744. Graphic Arts, The Sinclair Hamilton Collection.

· 1744 ·

Puritan morality was still strong in 1744. *The Progress of Sin, or, The Travels of Ungodliness* seen here includes a baleful portrait of the author as well as a full-page woodcut of Zion, the City of God, and its foes, including the Pope, the Emperor of Turkey, and an army of women of the City of Sensuality with "spotted faces, naked breasts and shoulders," described by Sinclair Hamilton as "a bevy of ladies in most *décolleté* costumes."

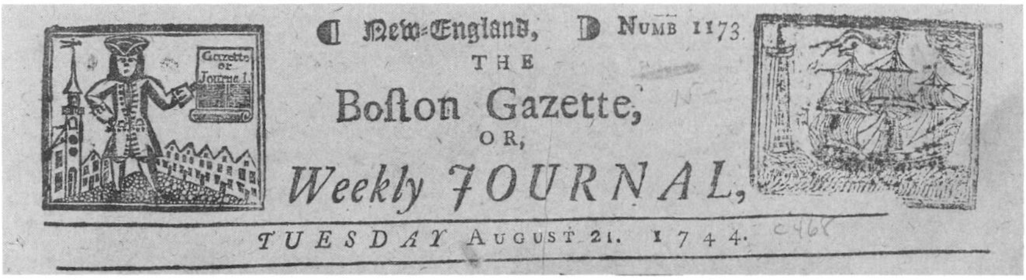

Masthead, *The Boston Gazette*. Boston, 1744. Graphic Arts, The Sinclair Hamilton Collection. (*detail*)

Masthead, *The American Magazine and Historical Chronicle*. Boston, 1745. Graphic Arts, The Sinclair Hamilton Collection. (*detail*)

· 1744–1745 ·

Primitive woodcuts prevail into the 1740s in the work of James Turner. Isaiah Thomas, the most important printer of the 1770s in New England, regarded Turner as the best picture engraver in the colonies. Turner favored type metal over wood and created miniature but visually strong cuts that were used as mastheads for two of Boston's earliest periodicals, the *American Magazine* and the *Boston Gazette*. Turner's naive but appealing cuts give us one of our earliest printed glimpse of Boston as well as what appears to be a colonial Boston newsboy peddling the *Gazette*.

Isaac Watts, *Sermon on Various Subjects, Divine and Moral....* Boston, 1746. Graphic Arts, The Sinclair Hamilton Collection.

· 1746 ·

The Boston *American Magazine* was highly praised by its readers for the quality of its printing. In 1746 Jonathan Edwards requested its printers, Rogers and Fowle, to print the sermons of Dr. Isaac Watts. The frontispiece was engraved for the *American Magazine* by James Turner, and is the first signed and dated copperplate portrait engraving in this country. Turner copied an earlier English engraving after a painting by Thomas Emmes, so that this labored image is at third hand from the original. Turner is much better in the naive but original imagery of the next book, *The History of the Holy Jesus.*

The History of the Holy Jesus. . . . Boston, 1749. Graphic Arts, The Sinclair Hamilton Collection.

· 1749 ·

Early American children's books present a fascinating history of their own. Beginning with the first New England primer, original sin, hell, and damnation are the main themes. Its ABC teaching of the alphabet indoctrinated every innocent soul with:

In Adam's Fall
We sinned All.

But by the 1749 publication of *The History of the Holy Jesus* the Puritan's soul-and-salvation fright had softened its tone, and the several woodcuts of this book, attributed to James Turner, are diminutive but irresistibly attractive invitations to the alphabet for young readers.

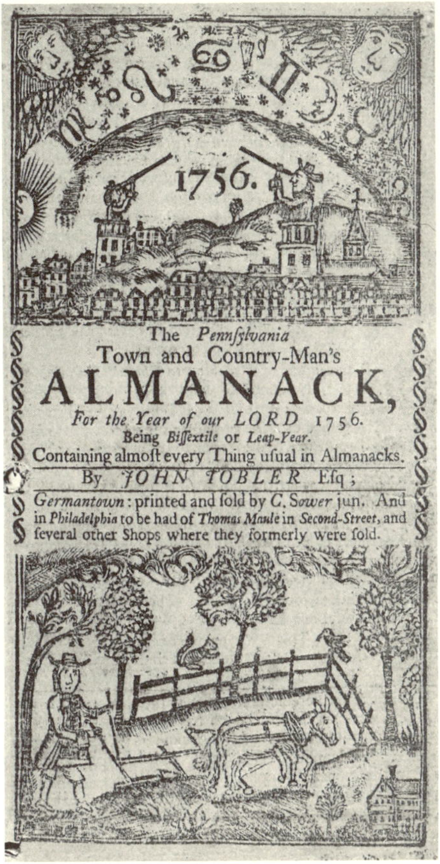

John Tobler, *The Pennsylvania Town and Country-Man's Almanack*. . . . Germantown, 1756. Graphic Arts, The Sinclair Hamilton Collection.

· 1756 ·

Primitive woodcut book illustration, like American primitive painting, offers great decorative charm. There is in such work an appealing expression of innocent wonder at the world. The pair of woodcuts that embellish this 1756 *Almanack*—possibly by James Turner—offers a delightful microcosm of early American town and country, encapsulating on one miniature page sun, moon, and stars, cherubim, the zodiac, two urban astronomers, and skyline towers representing city life. Below we find a happy farmer, plow and horse, clouds and trees, farm house, field, fence, chattering squirrel, and bird, decoratively summing up both town and country life on one slim octavo page.

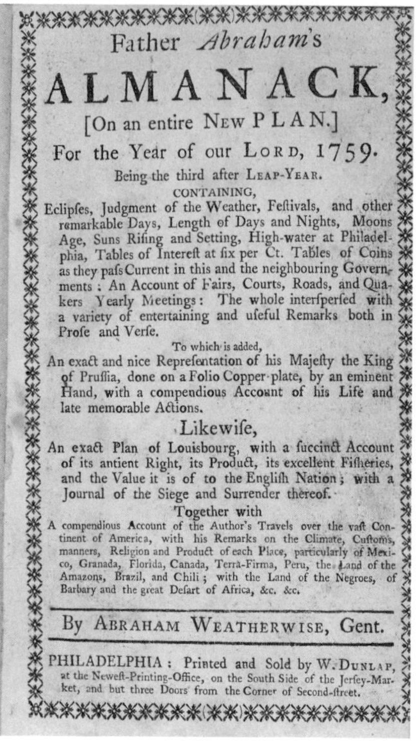
Father *Abraham's*

ALMANACK,

[On an entire NEW PLAN.]

For the Year of our LORD, 1759.

Being the third after LEAP-YEAR.

CONTAINING,

Eclipſes, Judgment of the Weather, Feſtivals, and other remarkable Days, Length of Days and Nights, Moons Age, Suns Riſing and Setting, High-water at Philadelphia, Tables of Intereſt at ſix per Ct. Tables of Coins as they paſs Current in this and the neighbouring Governments; An Account of Fairs, Courts, Roads, and Quakers Yearly Meetings: The whole interſperſed with a variety of entertaining and uſeful Remarks both in Proſe and Verſe.

To which is added,

An exact and nice Repreſentation of his Majeſty the King of Pruſſia, done on a Folio Copper-plate, by an eminent Hand, with a compendious Account of his Life and late memorable Actions.

Likewiſe,

An exact Plan of Louisbourg, with a ſuccinct Account of its antient Right, its Product, its excellent Fiſheries, and the Value it is of to the Engliſh Nation; with a Journal of the Siege and Surrender thereof.

Together with

A compendious Account of the Author's Travels over the vaſt Continent of America, with his Remarks on the Climate, Cuſtoms, manners, Religion and Product of each Place, particularly of Mexico, Granada, Florida, Canada, Terra-Firma, Peru, the Land of the Amazons, Brazil, and Chili; with the Land of the Negroes, of Barbary and the great Deſart of Africa, &c. &c.

By ABRAHAM WEATHERWISE, Gent.

PHILADELPHIA: Printed and Sold by W. DUNLAP, at the Neweſt-Printing-Office, on the South Side of the Jerſey-Market, and but three Doors from the Corner of Second-ſtreet.

Father Abraham's Almanack. . . . Philadelphia, 1759. Graphic Arts, The Sinclair Hamilton Collection.

· 1759 ·

Early American primitives, in printmaking as in painting, are usually anonymous. John Foster, James Franklin, and James Turner, already described, are among the few known by name. Another figure emerges after 1750 among Philadelphia imprints: Henry Dawkins. An apprentice to James Turner, Dawkins was one of the first American printmakers to work both wood and copper. His initials appear on several woodcuts, such as this beguiling scene of an astronomer (who has his telescope backwards). Dawkins, however, became mainly known through his copperplate work for bookplates, trade cards, and views. Long after copper-engraved prints were the standard illustration technique in Europe, primitive woodcuts were still the style for printed pictures in America. Copper engraving, with its far more sophisticated techniques and its demand for a heavy-pressure intaglio press, remained relatively rare in American prints.

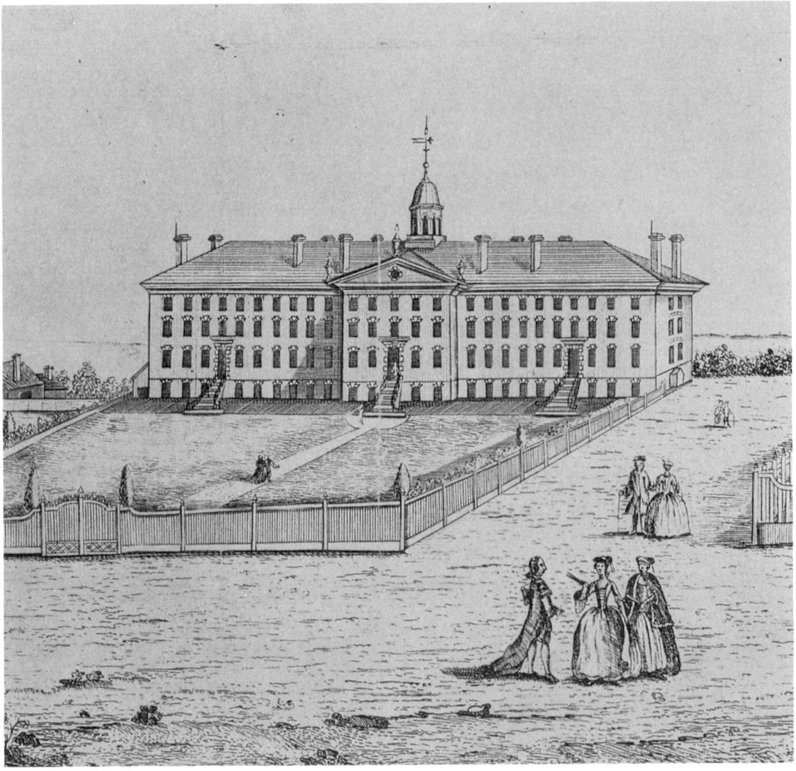

Henry Dawkins after William Tennant, *A North-West Prospect of Nassau Hall with a Front View of the President's House, in New Jersey.* Philadelphia, 1764. Rare Books. *(detail)*

· 1764 ·

"Aula Nassovica" had already appeared as an engraving in the *New American Magazine* for March, 1760. But a far more important view was engraved in 1764 by Henry Dawkins after a drawing by William Tennant, one of the earliest Princeton students, who graduated in 1758. Dawkins' copper engraving of Princeton is one of a group of college views that reflect increasing colonial pride in the slowly emerging civilization of America. Yale was pictured first in 1749, engraved by J. Greenwood, and Harvard by Paul Revere in 1768.

Henry Dawkins left Philadelphia for work in New York, where he succumbed to the early engraver's temptation to counterfeit the paper currency. In prison, and miserable, he made a famous plea for his own death penalty. Happily, Dawkins was pardoned and lived on working as an honest engraver until 1780.

Henry Bouquet, *An Historical Account of the Expedition Against the Ohio Indians*. . . . Philadelphia and London, 1766. Rare Books. Gift of Mrs. Marshall L. Brown.

· 1766 ·

The contrast between the long European tradition and the scant American tradition in the graphic arts, particularly copper engraving, is shown in an example illustrated in London by Benjamin West, our first great expatriate painter. Engraved in London by Pierre Canot after West's design and at almost the same time as Dawkins' Nassau Hall, we see skillfully rendered subtleties of tonality in the light and shade, graphic conventions of crosshatching and gradation of line totally lacking in the Dawkins work. Such technical virtuosity and stylistic elegance for American subjects created a conflict of aesthetic direction for American artists well through the next century.

Paul Sandby after Thomas Pownall, colored engraving, "A View of the Falls on the Passaick," from *Scenographia Americana*. London, 1768. Graphic Arts.

· 1768 ·

American scenery through European eyes is again exemplified in this early view of Passaic Falls in New Jersey. It conveys the same sense of wonder as Father Louis Hennepin's 1697 view of Niagara Falls. Both show grand American cataracts in a primeval world. More fantasy than reality, such prints are important as foreign visions of American iconography. The technical sophistication of the engraving by Paul Sandby gives the Passaic Falls and many of the twenty-eight other folio prints of *Scenographia Americana* a fascinating exoticism, recalling similar technical elegance of treatment in the sixteenth-century engravings of North America by Theodore de Bry.

Pierre Canot after Thomas Howdell, engraving, "South-East View of New York in North America," from *Scenographia Americana*. London, 1768. Graphic Arts. (*detail*)

· 1768 ·

Another plate from the *Scenographia* includes the earliest known view of King's College, now Columbia University, which was founded in 1754. The large palm tree in the foreground is not the Botanical Garden but artistic license by Howdell, who had never visited America and imagined it as a tropical paradise full of lush palms and waterfalls. Characteristically, this type of eighteenth-century view exploits the charm of European landscape engraving, which had become highly skilled but contains more style than substance. American primitives in copper engraving, such as those by Henry Dawkins and Paul Revere, are the opposite, with more concern for factual details than suavity of technique.

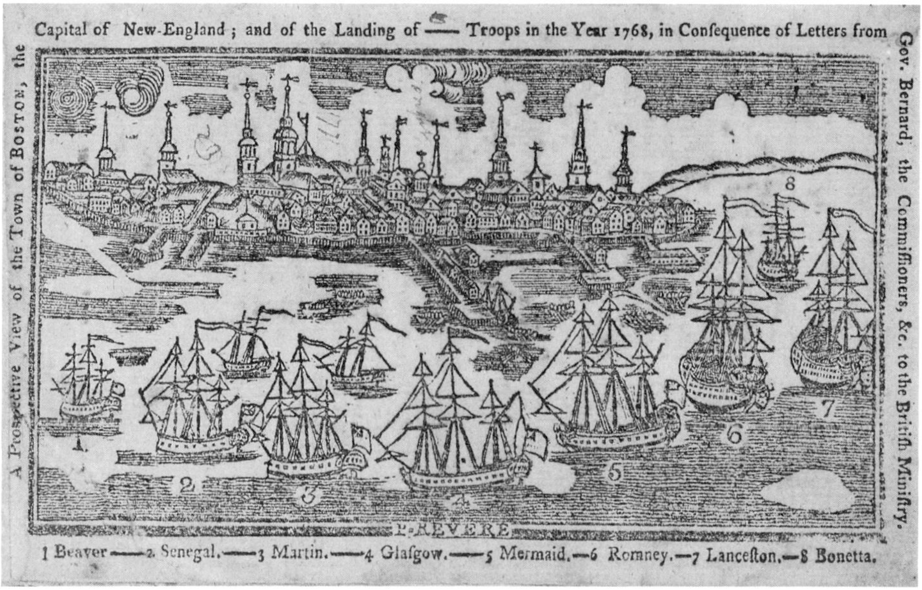

Paul Revere, woodcut, *A Prospective View of the Town of Boston, . . . and of the Landing of Troops in the Year 1768.* Boston, ca. 1768. Lent by Leonard L. Milberg, Class of 1953.

· 1768 ·

The anglicized visions seen in the *Scenographia Americana* do not reveal the rising rebellion in the American colonies at this time. By 1766 there were already signs of revolt in bold caricatures defying the many unfair taxes imposed by the crown. In order to defend unpopular tax laws and to increase the authority of the king, British warships and redcoat troops were sent to Boston harbor. Their arrival in 1768 was engraved by the Boston silversmith and patriot, Paul Revere, in both wood and copper. The ships, "their cannon loaded," encircled the harbor "as for a regular siege," writes Paul Revere. Their presence was offensive to the citizens of Boston, and fueled a protest that resulted in the "horrid massacre" of March, 1770, in which British soldiers fired on and killed five townsmen.

Paul Revere, hand-colored engraving, *The Bloody Massacre*. . . . Boston, 1770. The Scheide Library.

· 1770 ·

Few prints have influenced history as much as Paul Revere's engraving of the Boston Massacre of 1770. The fame of the print has obscured the fact that Revere actually plagiarized the image from a drawing of the horrible event made by Henry Pelham, half-brother of the American artist, John Singleton Copley. Revere recognized the propaganda value of the picture and "scooped" Pelham with his own crude copy, which appeared one week before Pelham's engraving. Revere's version of British soldiers firing on and killing unarmed citizenry had immediate emotional impact on the public, and was an initial incendiary spark that ignited the events leading to the American Revolution.

James Newton after William Pierrie, engraving, "A View of Boston taken on the Road to Dorchester," in *The Atlantic Neptune*. London, 1776. Lent by Leonard L. Milberg, Class of 1953. (*detail*)

· 1773 ·

Several drawings for an important atlas of maps and views of America were made in 1773 for the use of the British military, which would be engraved and published in London as *The Atlantic Neptune*. This work's serene aquatint views of Boston and New York belie the simmering unrest of the time. The "massacre" was still well remembered and the Boston Tea Party would soon occur. A prophetic letter from a "Gentleman of Character in London" was printed in the *New York Mercury* of 1773 saying: "I hear your Militia are put on a good footing, and that you are marching and counter-marching: it is well; but I am most desirous you should fortify; as sure as you live if you do not the town will be burnt around your ears in the next war, and in a couple of years or sooner such an Event is like to take place."*

* Quoted in Gloria-Gilda Deák, *Picturing America, 1497–1899. . . .*, 2 vols. (Princeton, 1988).

Carl Guttenberg after John Dixon's 1774 engraving, *Tea Tax Tempest, or the Anglo-American Revolution. . . .* Paris, ca. 1778. Graphic Arts. (*detail*)

· 1774 ·

This French copy of an English political cartoon is sharply observed European comment on the Boston Tea Party. Father Time projects his magic lantern show to four figures representing the four continents. They see with amazement the violent reaction caused by the new tea-tax in America. At the center, a tea pot explodes sending a snake, liberty cap, and pole flying. Beneath the cloud of smoke, the British lion sleeps. The caption of the English cartoon of 1774 remarks that the English "will smite themselves and will give America the means of siezing [*sic*] the Liberty Cap." By 1774 a congress of delegates from the colonies had met in Philadelphia in their first unified action. Two years later, in July 1776, Congress voted for independence.

The Royal American Magazine, or Universal Repository of Instruction and Amusement. Boston, 1774. Graphic Arts, The Sinclair Hamilton Collection.

· 1774 ·

The *Royal American Magazine* is full of the new rebellion, and the hand of several patriot heroes went into its publication. Isaiah Thomas, described by Benjamin Franklin as our "American Baskerville," was its editor and printer. He also edited, first in Boston and then in Worcester, the *Massachusetts Spy* with its militant "Liberty or Death—Join or Die" and "American Oracle of Liberty" headlines. Paul Revere contributed many of the *Royal American Magazine*'s patriotic engravings, including this crude copy of John Singleton Copley's portrait of John Hancock, embellished with the figure of Liberty.

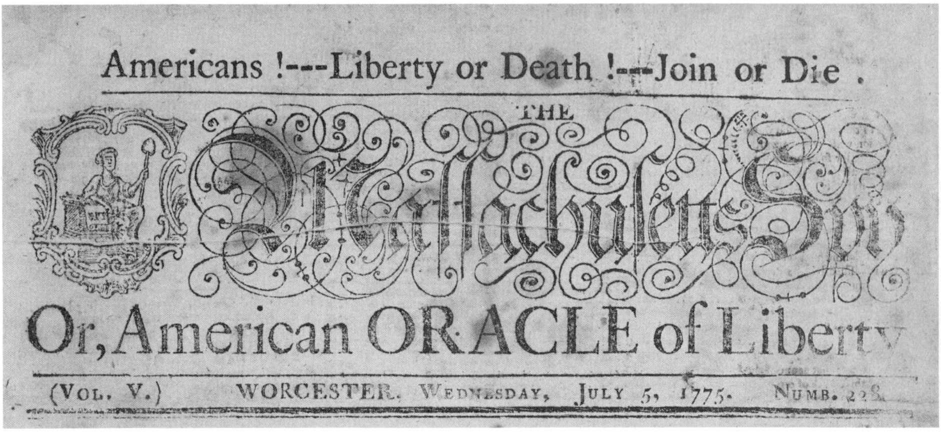

Masthead for *The Massachusetts Spy*. Worcester, Massachusetts, 1775.
Graphic Arts, The Sinclair Hamilton Collection. (*detail*)

· 1775 ·

Patriot printer Isaiah Thomas was in constant conflict with the royal government, and with the 1775 British occupation of Boston, he fled the city. Thomas not only helped Paul Revere rouse the countryside, but also fought in the battles of Lexington and Concord. Later that same month, April 1775, he set up the first press in Worcester and recommenced publication of his newspaper, the *Massachusetts Spy*. Isaiah Thomas as a printer would become even more influential than Benjamin Franklin. He published more than 400 works, later wrote the first and still definitive history of early American printing, and founded in 1812 the American Antiquarian Society in Worcester, Massachusetts.

IN CONGRESS, JULY 4, 1776.

A DECLARATION

BY THE REPRESENTATIVES OF THE

UNITED STATES OF AMERICA,

IN GENERAL CONGRESS ASSEMBLED.

WHEN in the Courſe of human Events, it becomes neceſſary for one People to diſſolve the Political Bands which have connected them with another, and to aſſume among the Powers of the Earth, the ſeparate and equal Station to which the Laws of Nature and of Nature's God entitle them, a decent Reſpect to the Opinions of Mankind requires that they ſhould declare the cauſes which impel them to the Separation.

WE hold theſe Truths to be ſelf-evident, that all Men are created equal, that they are endowed by their Creator with certain unalienable Rights, that among theſe are Life, Liberty, and the Purſuit of Happineſs---That to ſecure theſe Rights, Governments are inſtituted among Men, deriving their juſt Powers from the Conſent of the Governed, that whenever any Form of Government becomes deſtructive of theſe Ends, it is the Right of the People to alter or to aboliſh it, and to inſtitute new Government, laying its Foundation on ſuch Principles, and organizing its Powers in ſuch Form, as to them ſhall ſeem moſt likely to effect their Safety and Happineſs. Prudence, indeed, will dictate that Governments long eſtabliſhed ſhould not be changed for light and tranſient Cauſes; and accordingly all Experience hath ſhewn, that Mankind are more diſpoſed to ſuffer, while Evils are ſufferable, than to right themſelves by aboliſhing the Forms to which they are accuſtomed. But when a long Train of Abuſes and Uſurpations, purſuing invariably the ſame Object, evinces a Deſign to reduce them under abſolute Deſpotiſm, it is their Right, it is their Duty, to throw off ſuch Government, and to provide new Guards for their future Security. Such has been the patient Sufferance of theſe Colonies; and ſuch is now the Neceſſity which conſtrains them to alter their former Syſtems of Government. The Hiſtory of the preſent King of Great-Britain is a Hiſtory of repeated Injuries and Uſurpations, all having in direct Object the Eſtabliſhment of an abſolute Tyranny over theſe States. To prove this, let Facts be ſubmitted to a candid World.

HE has refuſed his Aſſent to Laws, the moſt wholeſome and neceſſary for the public Good.

HE has forbidden his Governors to paſs Laws of immediate and preſſing Importance, unleſs ſuſpended in their Operation till his Aſſent ſhould be obtained; and when ſo ſuſpended, he has utterly neglected to attend to them.

HE has refuſed to paſs other Laws for the Accommodation of large Diſtricts of People, unleſs thoſe People would relinquiſh the Right of Repreſentation in the Legiſlature, a Right ineſtimable to them, and formidable to Tyrants only.

HE has called together Legiſlative Bodies at Places unuſual, uncomfortable, and diſtant from the Depoſitory of their public Records, for the ſole Purpoſe of fatiguing them into Compliance with his Meaſures.

HE has diſſolved Repreſentative Houſes repeatedly, for oppoſing with manly Firmneſs his Invaſions on the Rights of the People.

HE has refuſed for a long Time, after ſuch Diſſolutions, to cauſe others to be elected; whereby the Legiſlative Powers, incapable of Annihilation, have returned to the People at large for their exerciſe; the State remaining in the mean time expoſed to all the Dangers of Invaſion from without, and Convulſions within.

HE has endeavoured to prevent the Population of theſe States; for that Purpoſe obſtructing the Laws for Naturalization of Foreigners; refuſing to paſs others to encourage their Migrations hither, and raiſing the Conditions of new Appropriations of Lands.

HE has obſtructed the Adminiſtration of Juſtice, by refuſing his Aſſent to Laws for eſtabliſhing Judiciary Powers.

HE has made Judges dependent on his Will alone, for the Tenure of their Offices, and the Amount and Payment of their Salaries.

HE has erected a Multitude of new Offices, and ſent hither Swarms of Officers to harraſs our People, and eat out their Subſtance.

HE has kept among us, in Times of Peace, Standing Armies, without the conſent of our Legiſlatures.

HE has affected to render the Military independent of and ſuperior to the Civil Power.

HE has combined with others to ſubject us to a Juriſdiction foreign to our Conſtitution, and unacknowledged by our Laws; giving his Aſſent to their Acts of pretended Legiſlation:

FOR quartering large Bodies of Armed Troops among us:

FOR protecting them, by a mock Trial, from Puniſhment for any Murders which they ſhould commit on the Inhabitants of theſe States:

FOR cutting off our Trade with all Parts of the World:

FOR impoſing Taxes on us without our Conſent:

FOR depriving us, in many Caſes, of the Benefits of Trial by Jury:

FOR tranſporting us beyond Seas to be tried for pretended Offences:

FOR aboliſhing the free Syſtem of Engliſh Laws in a neighbouring Province, eſtabliſhing therein an arbitrary Government, and enlarging its Boundaries, ſo as to render it at once an Example and fit Inſtrument for introducing the ſame abſolute Rule into theſe Colonies:

FOR taking away our Charters, aboliſhing our moſt valuable Laws, and altering fundamentally the Forms of our Governments:

FOR ſuſpending our own Legiſlatures, and declaring themſelves inveſted with Power to legiſlate for us in all Caſes whatſoever.

HE has abdicated Government here, by declaring us out of his Protection and waging War againſt us.

HE has plundered our Seas, ravaged our Coaſts, burnt our Towns, and deſtroyed the Lives of our People.

HE is, at this Time, tranſporting large Armies of foreign Mercenaries to compleat the Works of Death, Deſolation, and Tyranny, already begun with circumſtances of Cruelty and Perfidy, ſcarcely paralleled in the moſt barbarous Ages, and totally unworthy the Head of a civilized Nation.

HE has conſtrained our fellow Citizens taken Captive on the high Seas to bear Arms againſt their Country, to become the Executioners of their Friends and Brethren, or to fall themſelves by their Hands.

HE has excited domeſtic Inſurrections amongſt us, and has endeavoured to bring on the Inhabitants of our Frontiers, the mercileſs Indian Savages, whoſe known Rule of Warfare, is an undiſtinguiſhed Deſtruction, of all Ages, Sexes and Conditions.

IN every ſtage of theſe Oppreſſions we have Petitioned for Redreſs in the moſt humble Terms: Our repeated Petitions have been anſwered only by repeated Injury. A Prince, whoſe Character is thus marked by every act which may define a Tyrant, is unfit to be the Ruler of a free People.

NOR have we been wanting in Attentions to our Britiſh Brethren. We have warned them from Time to Time of Attempts by their Legiſlature to extend an unwarrantable Juriſdiction over us. We have reminded them of the Circumſtances of our Emigration and Settlement here. We have appealed to their native Juſtice and Magnanimity, and we have conjured them by the Ties of our common Kindred to diſavow theſe Uſurpations, which, would inevitably interrupt our Connections and Correſpondence. They too have been deaf to the Voice of Juſtice and of Conſanguinity. We muſt, therefore, acquieſce in the Neceſſity, which denounces our Separation, and hold them, as we hold the reſt of Mankind, Enemies in War, in Peace, Friends.

WE, therefore, the Repreſentatives of the UNITED STATES OF AMERICA, in GENERAL CONGRESS, Aſſembled, appealing to the Supreme Judge of the World for the Rectitude of our Intentions, do, in the Name, and by Authority of the good People of theſe Colonies, ſolemnly Publiſh and Declare, That theſe United Colonies are, and of Right ought to be, FREE AND INDEPENDENT STATES; that they are abſolved from all Allegiance to the Britiſh Crown, and that all political Connection between them and the State of Great-Britain, is and ought to be totally diſſolved; and that as FREE AND INDEPENDENT STATES, they have full Power to levy War, conclude Peace, contract Alliances, eſtabliſh Commerce, and to do all other Acts and Things which INDEPENDENT STATES may of right do. And for the ſupport of this Declaration, with a firm Reliance on the Protection of divine Providence, we mutually pledge to each other our Lives, our Fortunes, and our ſacred Honor.

Signed by ORDER *and in* BEHALF *of the* CONGRESS,

JOHN HANCOCK, PRESIDENT.

ATTEST.
CHARLES THOMSON, SECRETARY.

PHILADELPHIA: PRINTED BY JOHN DUNLAP.

John Dunlap, printer of the broadside, *A Declaration By the Representatives of the United States of America, In General Congress Assembled.* Philadelphia, 1776. The Scheide Library.

· 1776 ·

Through the combination of time, historic significance, and the peculiar aptness of their printing design, certain printed works present a visual mystique all their own. The Declaration of Independence broadside, with its well-spaced Caslon capitals, carefully chosen typography, and firm, well-inked impression, is the perfect American example of richly linked history and printed document. The pride of the printer, John Dunlap, comes through, keeping step with the powerful text. The first lines, in particular, mark a beginning in print like few others in history.

François Xavier Habermann. *Vue d'optique: Vue de Boston.* Augsburg, ca. 1776. Graphic Arts. (*detail*)

· 1776 ·

The American "Declaration of Independence" provoked immediate international response, and incidents in America were soon reported in several totally fanciful engravings created for the popular market in Europe. Among the most beguiling of these are the so-called *vues d'optiques*, which were meant to be seen on an optical device involving a special mirror and magnifying lens or "perspective glass." Some of the *vues d'optiques*, such as this one of Boston, were elaborately perforated and held up against the light to reveal lights and decorations, a forerunner in print for the first Fourth of July of illumination and fireworks.

François Xavier Habermann, colored engraving, *Vue d'Optique: La Destruction de la statue royale a Nouvelle Yorck*. Augsburg, ca. 1776. Graphic Arts. (*detail*)

· 1777 ·

Popular perspective views recorded additional historic events of the American war. Following John Dunlap's Philadelphia printing of the Declaration of Independence on July 4, copies were carried throughout the country, reaching Baltimore on July 9 and New York on July 10. As soon as soldiers and citizens in New York knew of the Declaration, they gathered in Bowling Green to pull down the hated symbol of British rule that stood there, the statue of George III.

Charles Willson Peale, oil on canvas, *George Washington after the Battle of Princeton*. Philadelphia, 1779–1782. The Wilson-Munn portrait, Princeton University. Gift of Charles Allen Munn, Class of 1881. ▶

· 1777 ·

Wars are among the best documented events in prints and drawings, and frequently the artists fought in the battles themselves. In America, two such gifted militiamen, Ralph Earl and Amos Doolittle, recorded with eyewitness precision the first military battles of the Revolution at Lexington and Concord in 1775. Colonial painter and soldier Charles Willson Peale was at the Battle of Princeton in January, 1777, and later he made several splendid paintings as well as a rare mezzotint print of General George Washington at the battle scene. Both paintings and print clearly show Nassau Hall in the midst of battle-smoke. It was a major target, and among the best stories of the engagement is that a cannonball entered one wall of Nassau Hall and pierced the painted portrait of George II. Only the gold frame survived. It now holds the celebrated portrait of General Washington at the Battle of Princeton, presumably painted by Peale to fit the frame.

In another Peale canvas, also at Princeton and now in the University Library, the smoke of battle has cleared above Nassau Hall. Washington stands at ease in a newly-donned uniform, his legs crossed and arm akimbo. His sword now sheathed, Washington is portrayed in the relaxed confidence of victory.

John Trumbull, wash drawing, *The Wounding of General Mercer at the Battle of Princeton.* Place unknown, ca. 1831. Graphic Arts, Iconography Collection. Gift of Junius Spencer Morgan, Class of 1888. (*detail*) ▶

· 1777 ·

The death of General Mercer was the most serious American loss at the Battle of Princeton. It became the dramatic central subject of John Trumbull's great historical painting in the rotunda of the Capitol in Washington, D.C., and a group of preparatory drawings for that painting are among the iconographic treasures of the Princeton University Library.

General Mercer was at the victory at Trenton on Christmas night, 1776. Later, on the march to Princeton on January 3, 1777, he and his troops were able to elude the British by taking a back road near what is now Mercer Street. But near the bridge at Stony Brook the British spotted them. Racing the British for higher ground, Mercer and his men were overtaken and surrounded. Mistaking Mercer for Washington, the British felled him.

The six drawings by Trumbull at Princeton reveal the artist's preoccupation over a period of many years with illustrating the theme, and demonstrate the evolution of his design from a tentative, careful outline to the highly dramatic, freely rendered drawing shown here.*

* Theodore Sizer, "Trumbull's *The Battle of Princeton*," *Princeton University Library Chronicle*, Vol. 12, No. 1 (Autumn 1950) 1–5.

James Peale, oil painting, *The Battle of Princeton*. Philadelphia?, no date. Graphic Arts, Iconography Collection. Gift of Dean Mathey, Class of 1912. (*detail*)

· ca. 1777 ·

James Peale, the younger brother of Charles Willson Peale, was also an officer under George Washington, and painted his own naive but vivid version of the Battle of Princeton. The death of General Mercer may again be seen in the center background. One version of Charles Willson Peale's full length portrait of Washington, the version commissioned in 1784 to hang in Nassau Hall, also shows the wounded General Mercer lying at Washington's feet. The artist's model for the General was Mercer's own son, Billy, who was an apprentice in the Peale studio while the picture was being painted. A deaf mute, Billy Mercer went on to become a painter and to make his own copy of this memorable Princeton battle scene by James Peale.*

* Now in the Historical Society of Pennsylvania. See Donald Drew Egbert, "General Mercer at the Battle of Princeton" *Princeton University Library Chronicle*, Vol. 13, No. 4, (Summer 1952) 171–194.

Pierre Eugene du Simitière, "George Washington," from *Thirteen Portraits of American Legislators, Patriots, and Soldiers, Who Distinguished Themselves in Rendering their Country Independent.* London, 1783. Rare Books, The Grenville Kane Collection.

· 1783 ·

A Swiss-born artist, antiquary, and lifelong collector of early Americana created the first printed portrait of George Washington. Pierre Eugene du Simitière left Europe in 1757 to travel to America, where he spent the rest of his life as a devoted but frustrated chronicler of his adopted country. In 1779 he drew the profile of Washington as the first of his series of "paper medals." Engraved in Paris by Prevost, the print became an instant popular favorite and was copied on everything from textiles to Wedgwood pottery. Du Simitière also opened his own "American Museum" in Philadelphia three years before Peale's much more famous establishment. Both of du Simitière's fervent endeavors, however, were financial disasters, and despite his lifelong efforts, he died a forgotten man in 1784.

Jean Baptiste Nini, intaglio dies used to cast terra cotta medallions of Benjamin Franklin. Paris, no date. Graphic Arts, Iconography Collection. Gift of Arthur C. Holden, Class of 1912.

· ca. 1783 ·

Following the war, the Continental Congress sent Benjamin Franklin to Paris as American minister to France. French sympathy for American independence became a love affair, and French artists—including Fragonard, Duplessis, Moreau le Jeune, and Jean Baptiste Nini—made the many sophisticated engravings, drawings, and medals now so familiar as Franklin imagery. Three terra cotta plaques made by Nini of *B. Franklin Americain* are wonderful eighteenth-century souvenirs of the great man, and show his profile first bareheaded, then with the freedom cap, and finally in the beaver fur hat that was such a particular hit with the French public.

Marguerite Gerard, etching after Jean Honoré Fragonard, *The Apotheosis of Franklin.* Paris, date unknown. Graphic Arts, Iconography Collection.

James Poupard, woodcut foldout sheet, *Metamorphosis*. Philadelphia, ca. 1783. Graphic Arts, The Sinclair Hamilton Collection.

· ca. 1783 ·

While elegant engravings of famous Americans were being done in France, the technique of American printmakers remained comparatively primitive. Wood, not copper, was the standard medium. Many woodcut-illustrated books and prints of this period are technically unskilled, but have their own rugged charm.

James Poupard was a native of Martinique who worked in Philadelphia and New York as an actor and printmaker. This signed "transformation" toy print has cut pages through the middle of the print. When lifted, the picture is "transformed" to a griffin, a woman, a mermaid, and a final skeleton emblematic of everyman's destination.

A Wonderful Discovery of a Hermit! Colored woodcut broadside. Place unknown, 1786. Graphic Arts, The Sinclair Hamilton Collection. *(detail)*

· 1786 ·

Woodcut broadsides of the eighteenth century were often the tabloid news of the day. Murders and hangings were vividly recorded, as well as such best-selling items as this discovery of a 200-year-old hermit at his cave by two wary foot soldiers. A companion second broadside shows a Dr. Brake visiting the old hermit and giving him his first glass of rum. The old hermit, who "might have lived 200 years more had he not drunk that horrid draught," died soon afterward.

Charles Willson Peale, engraving, "A N.W. View of the State House in Philadelphia," in *The Columbian Magazine, or, Monthly Miscellany.* Philadelphia, 1787. Rare Books.

· 1787–1789 ·

American copper engraving slowly began to appear as special frontispiece embellishment in such early American periodicals as the *Columbian Magazine* in Philadelphia and the *Massachusetts Magazine* in Boston. Charles Willson Peale's delineation of Independence Hall appeared in 1787, Samuel Hill's fine foldout engraving, "The State House in Boston," in 1789. Since copper engraving demanded the heavy pressure of a special intaglio press, these were expensive, luxurious additions to the presswork of the time.

Samuel Hill, engraving, "S.W. View of the State House in Boston," *The Massachusetts Magazine, or Monthly Museum. . . .* Boston, 1789. Graphic Arts, The Sinclair Hamilton Collection. (*detail*) ▶

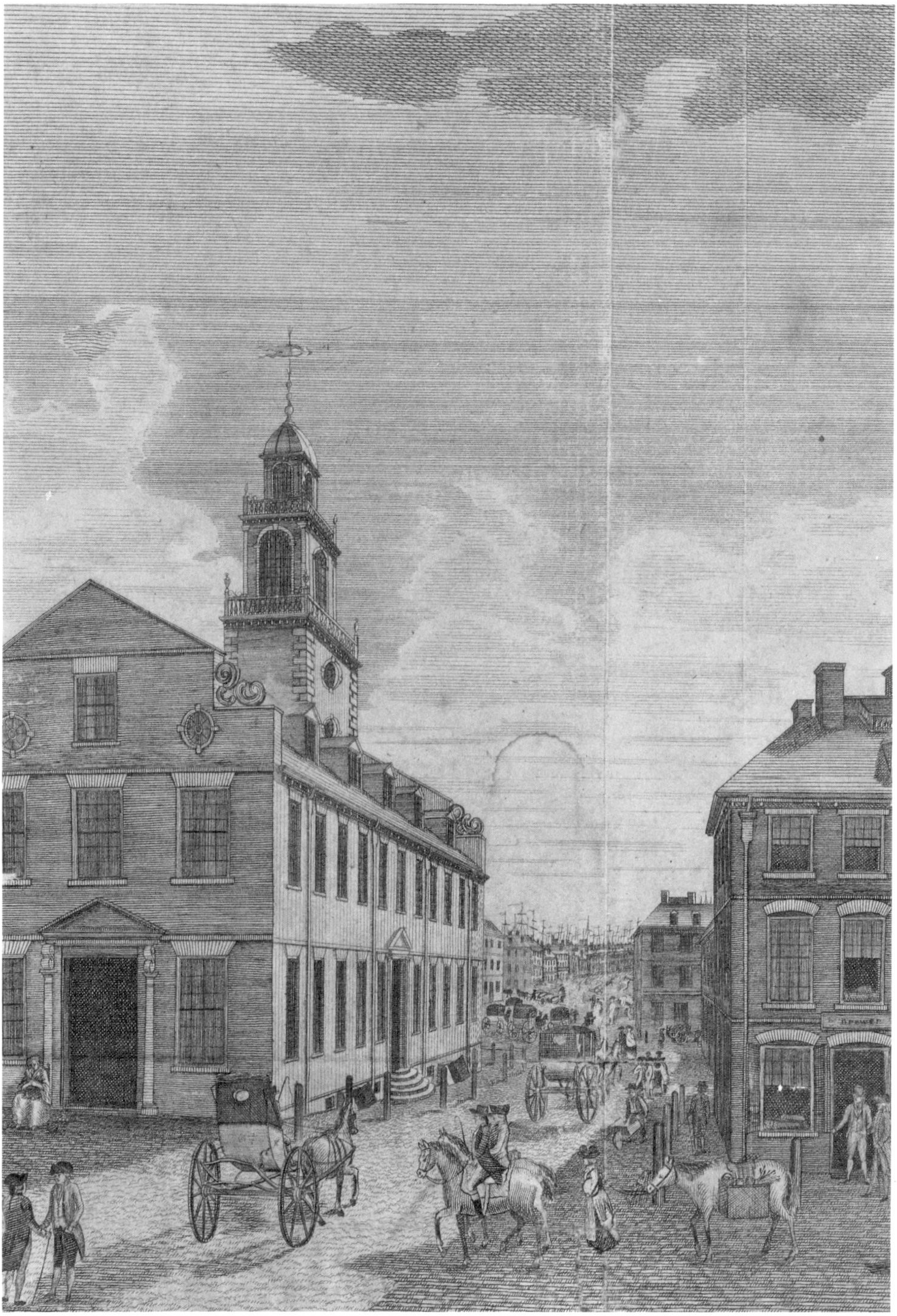

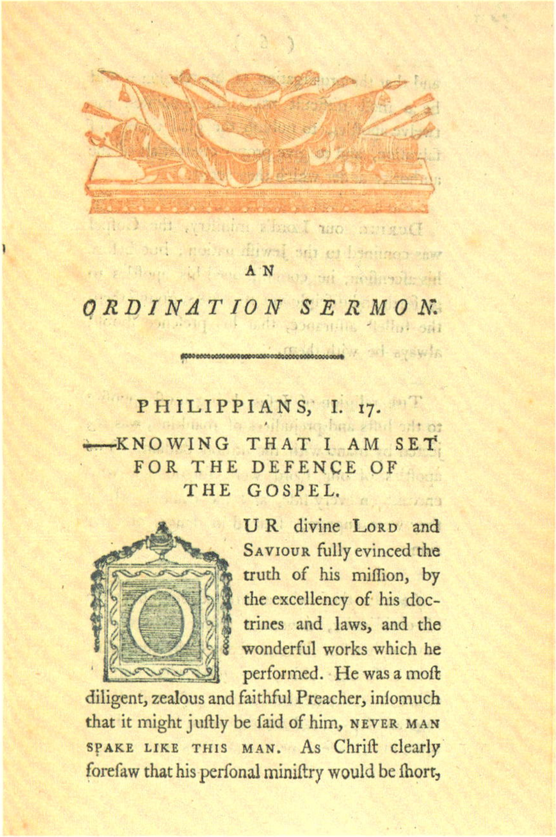
AN

ORDINATION SERMON.

PHILIPPIANS, I. 17.

—KNOWING THAT I AM SET FOR THE DEFENCE OF THE GOSPEL.

OUR divine LORD and SAVIOUR fully evinced the truth of his miſſion, by the excellency of his doctrines and laws, and the wonderful works which he performed. He was a moſt diligent, zealous and faithful Preacher, inſomuch that it might juſtly be ſaid of him, NEVER MAN SPAKE LIKE THIS MAN. As Chriſt clearly foreſaw that his perſonal miniſtry would be ſhort,

John Mycall, printer, page from *A Sermon delivered December 10, 1788, at the Ordination of the Rev. John Andrews*. Newburyport, Massachusetts, 1789. Graphic Arts, The Sinclair Hamilton Collection.

· 1789 ·

Color printing demands special attention from the printer to solve not only technical problems of inking and register, but also difficult aesthetic decisions. Among the first printers in America to deal with these graphic design concerns was John Mycall of Newburyport, Massachusetts. Mycall adopted a French approach to his typographic style, as opposed to the English look of most early American books. He liberally used printers' fleurons and decorative headpieces in the French style, and in this rare example presents the reader with the first multicolor printing in America, appropriately enough in the Franco-American tricolor of red, white, and blue.

THE
COLUMBIAN MAGAZINE,
OR,
MONTHLY MISCELLANY.
For JUNE, 1789.

PHILADELPHIA: PRINTED FOR JAMES TRENCHARD,
BY TRENCHARD AND STEWART,
At their PRINTING-OFFICE, East Side of Water Street, between Chesnut and Walnut Streets; where all Kinds of Printing is done with neatness and dispatch, and on the most reasonable terms.
Subscriptions are taken in by the principal Booksellers in Pennsylvania—Mr. Samuel Campbell, and Messrs. Berry and Rogers, in New-York—Mr. Hall, Boston.—Mr. I. Beers, New-Haven—Messrs. Spotswood and Clarke, Baltimore—Mr. Dewees, Messrs. F. and S. Green, Annapolis—Mr. A. Davis, Richmond—At No. 24, Broad-street, Charleston, South-Carolina—P. Hearne, Savannah.

The Columbian Magazine, or, Monthly Miscellany. Philadelphia, 1789. Graphic Arts.

· 1789 ·

A stirring of new patriotic pride becomes evident in the 1780s when Joel Barlow wrote his "Vision of Columbus" that would become his famous *Columbiad* of 1807. At about the same time, Yale's president, Timothy Dwight, was inspired to personify America as the goddess Columbia (changing the gender of Columbus). It was a symbol that gave a new pride in American history as the nation approached 1792 and the tercentenary of its discovery. The *Columbian Magazine* cover of 1789 flourished an early emblem of the American eagle perched atop the globe and surrounded not only by shield, anchor, and plow, but also by the lyre and book, traditional emblems for music and learning.

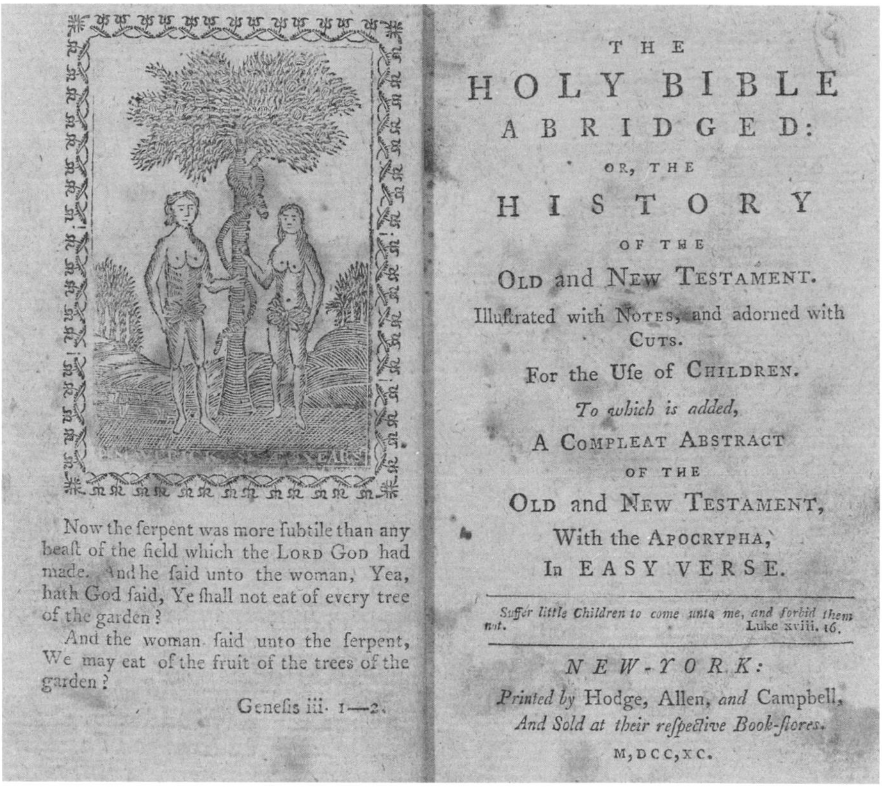

Now the ferpent was more fubtile than any beaft of the field which the LORD GOD had made. And he faid unto the woman, Yea, hath God faid, Ye fhall not eat of every tree of the garden?

And the woman faid unto the ferpent, We may eat of the fruit of the trees of the garden?

Genefis iii. 1—2.

THE
HOLY BIBLE
ABRIDGED:
OR, THE
HISTORY
OF THE
OLD and NEW TESTAMENT.
Illuftrated with NOTES, and adorned with CUTS.
For the Ufe of CHILDREN.
To which is added,
A COMPLEAT ABSTRACT
OF THE
OLD and NEW TESTAMENT,
With the APOCRYPHA,
In EASY VERSE.

Suffer little Children to come unto me, and forbid them not. Luke xviii. 16.

NEW-YORK:
Printed by Hodge, Allen, *and* Campbell,
And Sold at their refpective Book-ftores.
M,DCC,XC.

The Holy Bible Abridged; or, The History of the Old and New Testament . . . For the Use of Children. New York, 1790. Graphic Arts, The Sinclair Hamilton Collection.

· 1790 ·

The Maverick family produced several of the most productive of early American engravers, with more than 2,000 engravings to their credit.* Peter Rushton Maverick, the father of the clan, taught the engraver's trade to his two sons, Peter and Samuel, who in turn taught their several children. The elder son, Peter, became the more successful and taught Asher Durand, among many others. Peter Maverick's first juvenile work, a wood engraving, appears here, proudly signed "P. Maverick, sc.ae. [*sculpsit aetatis*, or engraved at age] 9 years."

* Stephen DeWitt Stephens, *The Mavericks* (New Brunswick, New Jersey, 1950).

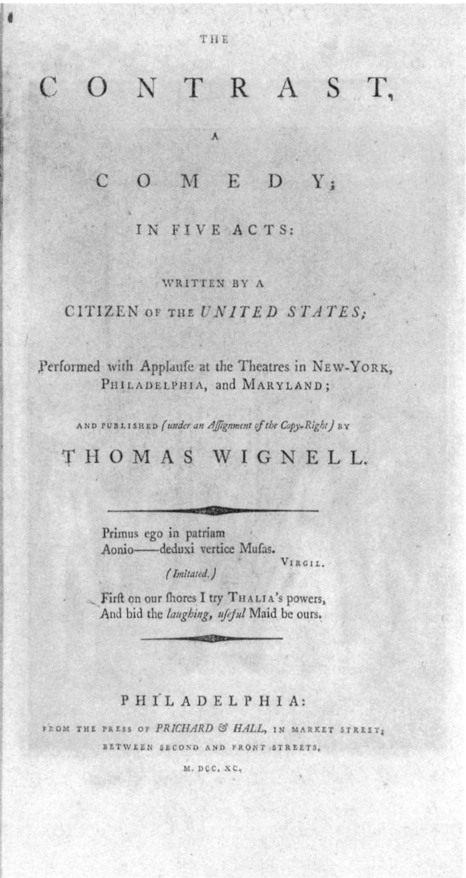
THE
CONTRAST,
A
COMEDY;
IN FIVE ACTS:

WRITTEN BY A
CITIZEN OF THE *UNITED STATES;*

Performed with Applaufe at the Theatres in NEW-YORK, PHILADELPHIA, and MARYLAND;

AND PUBLISHED *(under an Affignment of the Copy-Right)* BY
THOMAS WIGNELL.

Primus ego in patriam
Aonio——deduxi vertice Mufas.
VIRGIL.
(Imitated.)
Firft on our fhores I try THALIA's powers,
And bid the *laughing, ufeful* Maid be ours.

PHILADELPHIA:
FROM THE PRESS OF *PRICHARD & HALL*, IN MARKET STREET,
BETWEEN SECOND AND FRONT STREETS.
M. DCC. XC.

Royall Tyler, *The Contrast, a Comedy in Five Acts. . . .* Philadelphia, 1790. Rare Books. Gift of Robert Williams, Class of 1915.

· 1790 ·

In the same year that his nine-year-old son first appeared in print, the elder Maverick engraved the frontispiece of the first play written and performed in America, Royall Tyler's *The Contrast.* Federal-period culture was becoming manifest in all the arts, particularly in Philadelphia, the new "Athens of America." The play also asserted American independence from European culture, contrasting the well-travelled but foppish Billy Dimple with the unpolished but honorable American, Colonel Manly (played by the early American actor, John Henry).

James Trenchard (?), engraving after William Bartram, "Andromeda pulverulenta," in Bartram's *Travels through North and South Carolina, Georgia, East and West Florida.* Philadelphia, 1791. Rare Books.

· 1791 ·

John Bartram was one of the original members of Benjamin Franklin's American Philosophical Society in Philadelphia. The Society believed, as Franklin wrote, that "the first drudgery" of settling the new colonies "was now pretty well over" and that the time had come "to cultivate the fine Arts, and improve the common stock of Knowledge." One of the first Americans to carry this philosophy forward was John Bartram's son William, who, following Mark Catesby, was one of the earliest artist-naturalists to publish drawings of American flora and fauna. William Bartram's *Travels*, published in Philadelphia in 1791, included several sensitive drawings by the author. The engraver well may have been James Trenchard, a close friend of Charles Willson Peale and publisher of the *Columbian Magazine.*

Edward Savage, mezzotint engraving after Charles Willson Peale, *Portrait of David Rittenhouse*. Philadelphia, 1796. Graphic Arts. (*detail*)

· 1796 ·

David Rittenhouse was a Philadelphia instrument-maker and astronomer whose name is well known at Princeton for his orrery, or mechanical model of the solar system, made for the college in 1767. This beautiful scientific model is well preserved and now may be seen in Peyton Hall, the astronomy building on campus. Rittenhouse was a good example in Philadelphia of those who had been influenced by the Enlightenment. In 1791, when he was made president of the American Philosophical Society, he sat for the portrait by Charles Willson Peale, seen here in Edward Savage's mezzotint engraving.

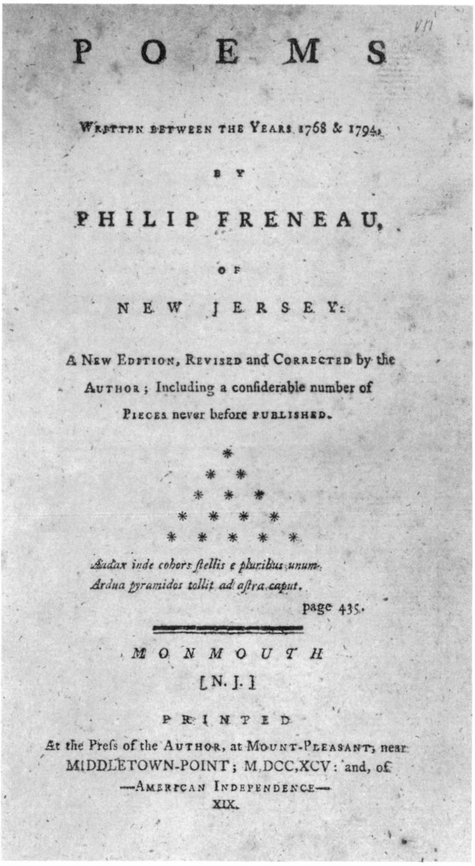

POEMS

WRITTEN BETWEEN THE YEARS 1768 & 1794,

BY

PHILIP FRENEAU,

OF

NEW JERSEY:

A NEW EDITION, REVISED and CORRECTED by the AUTHOR; Including a conſiderable number of PIECES never before PUBLISHED.

*
* *
* * *
* * * *
* * * * *

Audax inde cohors ſtellis e pluribus unum,
Ardua pyramidos tollit ad aſtra caput.
page 435.

MONMOUTH
[N. J.]

PRINTED

At the Preſs of the AUTHOR, at MOUNT-PLEASANT, near MIDDLETOWN-POINT; M,DCC,XCV: and, of
—AMERICAN INDEPENDENCE—
XIX.

Philip Freneau, *Poems*. . . . Monmouth, N[ew] J[ersey], 1795. Rare Books.

· 1795 ·

Nationalism and culture also found expression in early American poetry. Two Princeton undergraduates, Philip Freneau and Hugh Henry Brackenridge, wrote a fervid poetic essay on "The Rising Glory of America," which was read at the Princeton Commencement of 1771. It included the lines "Paradise anew shall flourish, by the second Adam lost." Freneau became known as the "poet of the American Revolution." By 1795 he had settled in Monmouth, New Jersey, where he created his own press at Point Pleasant to print a collected edition of his poems. The title page shows surprising typographic sensitivity, and is dated "American Independence XIX."

James Sharples, pastel drawing, *Samuel Stanhope Smith.* Princeton, 1795. Graphic Arts, Iconography Collection.

· 1795 ·

From about 1793 to 1801 an English pastel artist, James Sharples, and his family were in Philadelphia and New York as travelling portrait painters. Their small, highly skilled pastel drawings became an essential part of almost every fashion-conscious household of the day, leaving us a remarkably graceful "national portrait gallery" of American citizens of the last decade of the eighteenth century. James Sharples also came to Princeton, where in 1795 he drew the new president of the College of New Jersey, Samuel Stanhope Smith, Class of 1769. Aside from this fine pastel drawing, Smith's presidency (1795–1812) is remembered not only for his major educational reforms, but also for the terrible fire of 1804 that almost destroyed Nassau Hall, and for the student riot of 1807, after which 125 of the 200 students at the College were expelled.

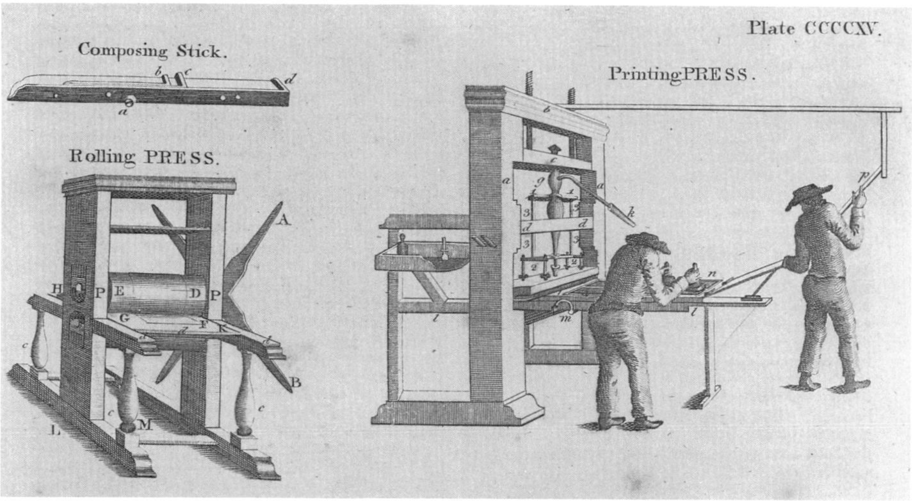

Thomas Dobson, *Encyclopaedia Britannica*, third issue, 18 vols. Philadelphia, 1790–1797. Rare Books. (*detail*)

· 1790–1797 ·

The Enlightenment in Philadelphia was given nationalistic expression by the publication of an independent American edition of the *Encyclopaedia Britannica*. This American edition was completed in 1797 in 18 volumes, some 15,400 pages, and 540 engraved plates. It was printed on paper hand-made in Pennsylvania, with type cast in Philadelphia. The printer, Thomas Dobson, maintained the best typographic quality throughout, and employed most of the engravers in Philadelphia to illustrate this monument of intellectual and graphic enterprise. Dobson's achievement marked "the end of printing as a household craft and the beginning of its factory stage of development."*

* Lawrence C. Wroth, *The Colonial Printer* (New York, 1931), p. 294.

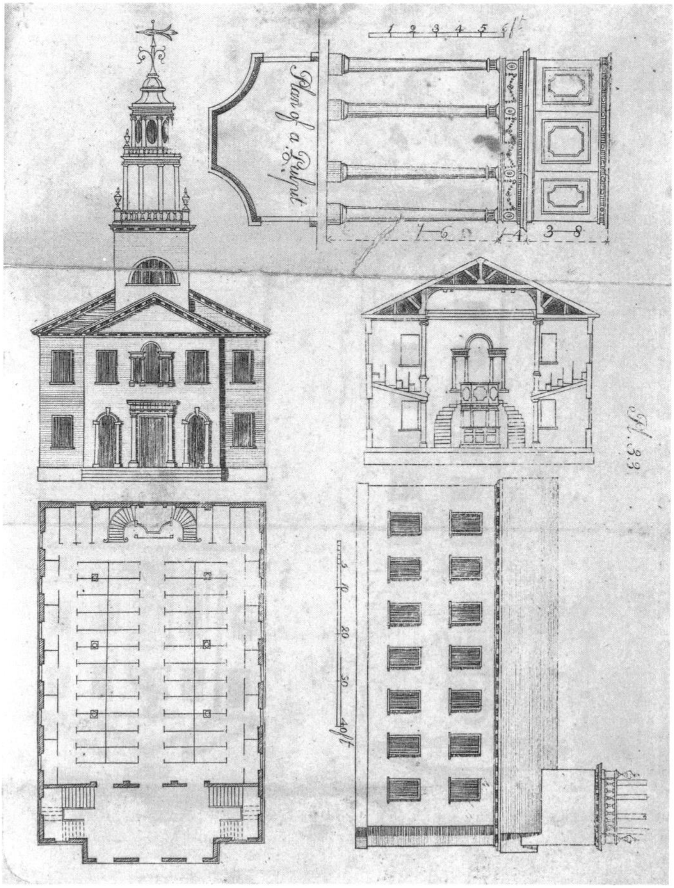

Asher Benjamin, *The Country Builder's Assistant.* . . . Worcester, Massachusetts, 1798. Graphic Arts, The Sinclair Hamilton Collection.

· 1798 ·

The earliest of many printed guides for carpenters and builders, Asher Benjamin's *The Country Builder's Assistant* is the first of seven books he published between 1797 and 1845. First issued in Greenfield, Massachusetts, in 1797, it was followed by the Worcester edition of 1798, showing the quick spread of this work throughout New England. The book also helped establish excellent and uniform Georgian taste in American architecture in the late eighteenth century. So few New England towns of the period escaped its influence that much of the pervasive New England look of the Federal period may be credited to Asher Benjamin.

William Nutter, color printed engraving after Gilbert Stuart, *Geo. Washington Esqr.* London, 1798. Graphic Arts.

· 1798 ·

Gilbert Stuart, one of the most celebrated American artists of the eighteenth century, studied in London with Benjamin West for six years. He returned to America in 1792 and a decade later he was the reigning portrait painter of his day. His fame was firmly established with three life portraits of George Washington. The most familiar of these, the Athenaeum Portrait painted in 1796, has become an almost inescapable American icon, appearing—among innumerable other places—on our one-dollar bill. This William Nutter engraving after Stuart's painting is a rare English work printed in colors from the plate, and published the year before Washington's death in 1799.

NINETEENTH CENTURY

William Russell Birch, colored engraving, *Second Street North from Market St. with Christ Church*. Philadelphia, 1800–1801. Graphic Arts. Gift of William Prickett, Class of 1947.

· 1800 ·

William Russell Birch was an established artist and engraver in London before coming to America in 1795. Settling in Philadelphia, he soon produced the most attractive illustrated book to be created by that time in America, *The City of Philadelphia . . . As it Happened in the Year 1800*. Working with his gifted son Thomas, he quickly sold out the three editions that appeared in 1800–1801, 1804, and 1827. It is the first of many series of city views that would be produced in America, and portrays a city of grace and style to rival the much older European cities of Paris and London. The population of Philadelphia had doubled since 1790, surpassing New York and Boston as the largest city in America for much of the nineteenth century.

William Russell Birch, colored engraving, *The City of Philadelphia in the State of Pennsylvania.* Philadelphia, 1801. Lent by Leonard L. Milberg, Class of 1953.

· 1801 ·

William Russell Birch created two folio prints—one of New York and one of Philadelphia—as a special promotional advertisement for his series of Philadelphia views. The advertisement displays the artist's pleasure in his work, saying of these two prints "[the artist] . . . flatters himself [they] will surpass anything of the kind yet published in this country . . . [and they are] intended as elegant furniture for a drawing or sitting room. . . . " Birch's Philadelphia view is indeed elegant, framed by the luxuriant branches of the great elm at Kensington, known as "William Penn's Tree." The tree, made famous by Penn's treaty with the Indians, was destroyed in a storm a few years after Birch's print was made.

Thomas Clarke, stipple engraving, *Sacred to the Memory of the Illustrious G. Washington.* Boston, 1801. Graphic Arts.

· 1801 ·

The death of George Washington in 1799 led to an outpouring of national grief. In this engraved memorial print the figure of Liberty comforts two disconsolate visitors to his tomb, inscribed "There is Rest in Heaven." Similar sentiments inspired countless silk-stitched embroideries and other *memento mori* for the loss of the Father of the Country. The technique employed in this print, stipple engraving, uses dots rather than line to create its image, and was a recent highly fashionable development in English printmaking.

William Russell Birch, colored engraving, *High Street, From the Country Market-place, Philadelphia: with the Procession in Commemoration of the Death of General George Washington....* Philadelphia, 1804. Graphic Arts. Gift of William Prickett, Class of 1947.

· 1804 ·

This somber view of George Washington's funeral procession was drawn and engraved as one of a series of *Views of Philadelphia* by William Russell Birch and first published on December 31, 1800. Many of the plates for this album were reworked by Birch, so that this 1804 second-state print has had one figure removed, a weeping mourner usually seen on the far right of this image. Burnishing and polishing the copper plate erases any lines the engraver may wish to omit, but the ghostly figure of the mourner is still faintly visible here.

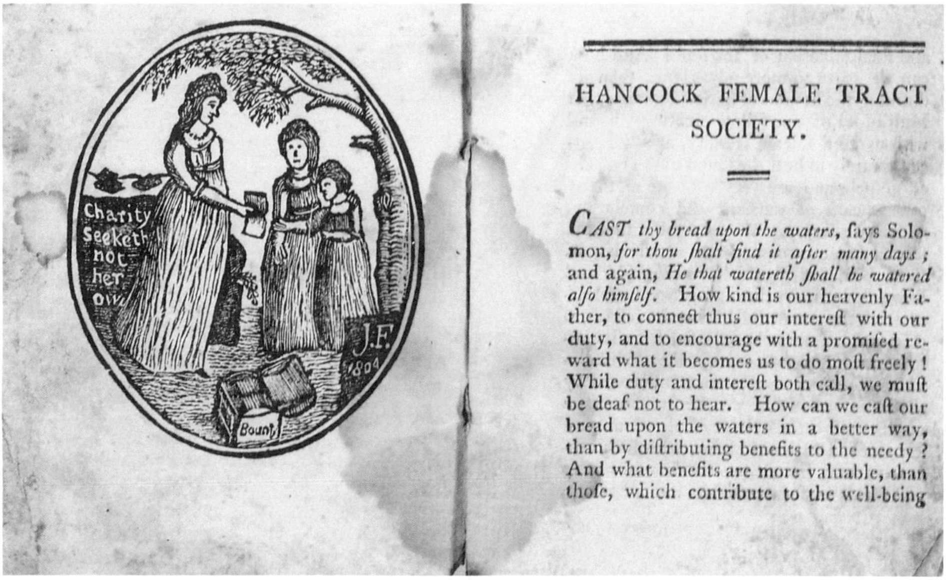

HANCOCK FEMALE TRACT SOCIETY.

CAST thy bread upon the waters, ſays Solomon, *for thou ſhalt find it after many days*; and again, *He that watereth ſhall be watered alſo himſelf.* How kind is our heavenly Father, to connect thus our intereſt with our duty, and to encourage with a promiſed reward what it becomes us to do moſt freely! While duty and intereſt both call, we muſt be deaf not to hear. How can we caſt our bread upon the waters in a better way, than by diſtributing benefits to the needy? And what benefits are more valuable, than thoſe, which contribute to the well-being

Jonathan Fisher, *Hancock Female Tract Society.* Sedgwick, Maine, 1804.
Graphic Arts, The Sinclair Hamilton Collection.

· 1804 ·

The early nineteenth century produced some remarkable inventors and thinkers well-characterized as blessed with "Yankee ingenuity." The type is seen in several early self-taught printmakers, including Amos Doolittle and Abel Buell of Connecticut, and Jonathan Fisher of Maine. The versatile Fisher was a Harvard graduate, then a celebrated minister in Blue Hill, Maine, where he was also well known as a poet, linguist, farmer, furniture maker, printer on his own press, binder, and engraver on wood. This small religious tract is the first signed and dated book printed, bound, and illustrated by Fisher (see also 1807).

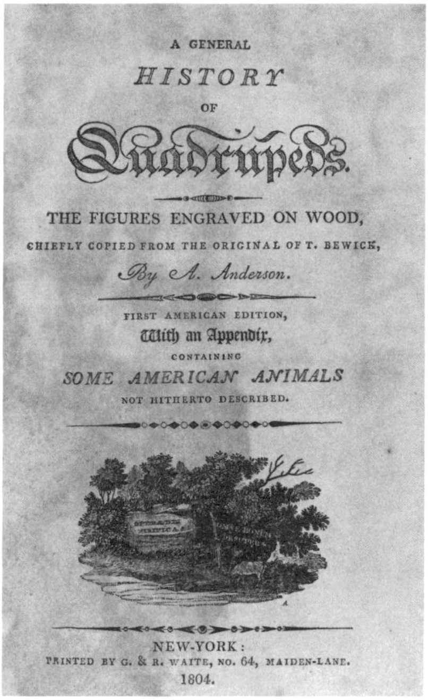

Alexander Anderson, two wood-engraved trade cards, and title page, *A General History of Quadrupeds . . . with an Appendix Containing Some American Animals. . . .* New York, 1804. Graphic Arts, The Sinclair Hamilton Collection.

· 1804 ·

Called the father of wood engraving in America, Alexander Anderson was the first printmaker to adopt a technique newly developed by Thomas Bewick in England: the engraving in white line on end-grain wood, rather than the relatively crude cutting on the cross grain, a technique used throughout the world for woodcut pictures before Bewick's invention. In 1804 Anderson demonstrated his devotion to Bewick by printing an American edition of Bewick's *A General History of Quadrupeds* (Newcastle upon Tyne, 1790) with his own re-engraved blocks, and "some American animals not hitherto described." Anderson's influence in the continuation of a strong English look to American book illustration was pervasive, since he lived throughout most of the century and taught several other important engravers to work in the English Bewick style, including Garrett Lansing, John Hall, and William Morgan.

William Constable, watercolor drawing, inscribed, *Mill at Parkman Town on the Head of the Grand River, Emptying into Lake Erie.* Parkman Town, Pennsylvania, 1806. Graphic Arts. Gift of Leonard L. Milberg, Class of 1953.

· 1806 ·

Early nineteenth-century travellers to America from abroad often kept diaries which, at their best, are illustrated with drawings descriptive of the local scenery. Such travel sketches have a long tradition extending back to Jacques Le Moyne and John White, and continued early in the nineteenth century by such observers as the Baroness Anne Margueritte Hyde de Neuville, Pavel Svinin, and William Constable. Constable was a Scotsman who toured the United States in 1806 making many delicate watercolors of what he saw. At Trenton, New Jersey, he drew "Bridge on the Delaware," and near Lake Erie in Pennsylvania he painted "The Mill at Parkman Town." Such water-mills were long an essential part of the economy, particularly in the papermaking industry, and were an integral part of the early nineteenth-century American industrial scene.

Robert Fulton, watercolor drawing, *Love's First Interview.* New York, 1806. Graphic Arts.

· 1806 ·

Chiefly remembered for inventing an early diving boat called *Nautilus* and a highly successful steamboat he called the *Clermont*, Robert Fulton was a professional painter of miniatures and portraits for many years before he turned to engineering. He resided in England from 1786 until he returned to New York in 1806. In that year this intimate little scene was painted, and it is tempting to think of it as autobiographical, and that the admiring swain might even be a self-portrait.

Jonathan Fisher, oil painting on wood, *Nassau Hall*. Blue Hill, Maine?, 1807. Graphic Arts, Iconography Collection. Gift of a Group of Alumni. (*detail*)

· 1807 ·

Although he never visited Princeton, self-taught artist Jonathan Fisher seems to have been so impressed with Nassau Hall that he created a large and truly remarkable oil painting of the architectural centerpiece of the College of New Jersey. He must have seen or purchased a copy of the 1764 engraving by Henry Dawkins, for it is a direct copy of that print. A painting copied from a print is a reversal of the usual painter-engraver roles, and Fisher's painting turns Dawkins' awkward design into a far more generous artistic statement.

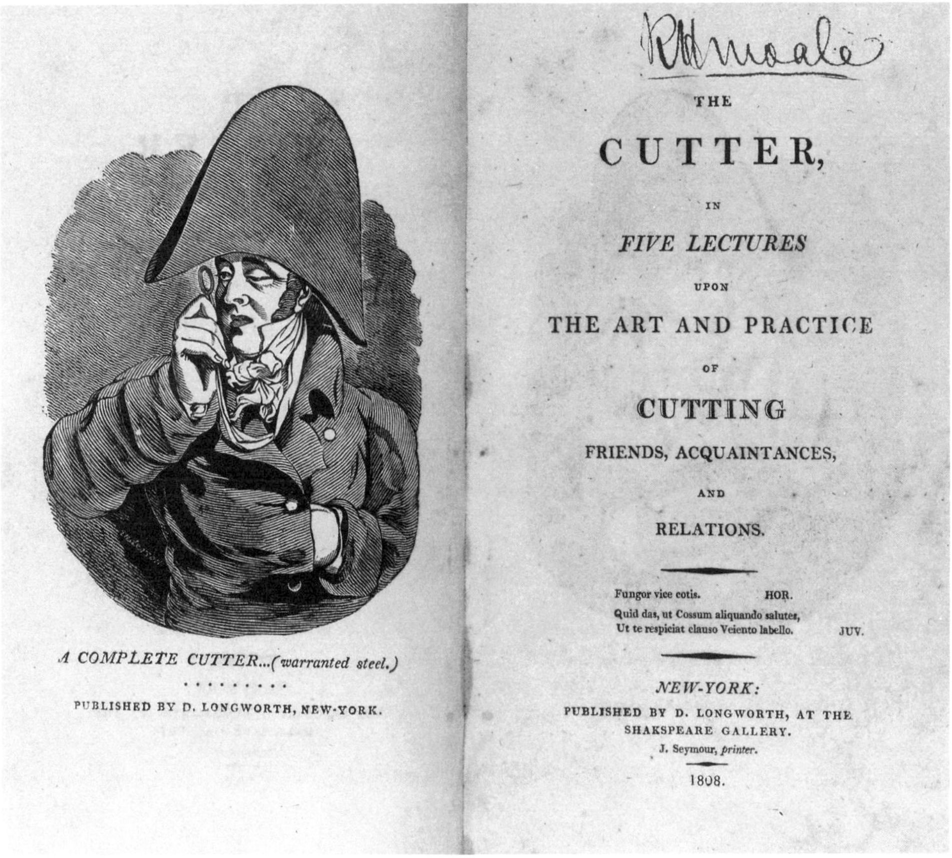

Alexander Anderson, "A Complete Cutter . . . (warranted steel)," in Arthur Benoni Evans, *The Cutter, in Five Lectures upon the Art and Practice of Cutting Friends, Acquaintances, and Relations.* New York, 1808. Graphic Arts, The Sinclair Hamilton Collection.

· 1808 ·

A new class-conscious society in New York City began to express itself in such books as this manual on how to be a professional snob. It is full of sharply satirical advice: "The word 'Sir,' with an appropriate intonation of the voice, has a wonderful effect to chill the forward and importunate and may be said when accompanied by a frigid inclination of the head . . . to amount to a '*dead cut.*'" Alexander Anderson provided the wood engraving for the book's frontispiece (see also 1804).

Charles Balthazar Julien Fevret de Saint-Mémin, engraved profiles of Thomas Jefferson and Langdon Carter. Place unknown, 1808. Graphic Arts, Iconography Collection. Gift of Clara M. Kirk and of Rudolph Kirk, Class of 1922.

· 1808 ·

The unusual number of profile portraits of early Americans was partly the result of the fashion of the time, but in larger part it was a matter of practicality. Capturing a likeness is far simpler in a profile, and for Saint-Mémin even mechanized through the use of an invention called the *physiognotrace*. This contrivance actually traced the sitter's profile onto a screen, which was then miniaturized by pantograph and "finished" by the artist. Saint-Mémin was particularly adept at the finishing details, giving marvelous life to the otherwise contrived image. He offered an attractive package to his clients, including a life-sized drawing on pink paper, framed in his own gold and black design, the miniaturized engraved plate, and an edition of prints pulled from the plate.

Charles Balthazar Julien Fevret de Saint-Mémin, pastel drawing of Langdon Carter. Place unknown, 1808. Graphic Arts, Iconography Collection. Gift of Clara M. Kirk and of Rudolph Kirk, Class of 1922.

Alexander Wilson, *American Ornithology: or, The Natural History of the Birds of the United States*, 9 volumes. Philadelphia, 1808–1814. Rare Books. (*detail*)

· 1808 ·

The recognition of indigenous species, particularly for American birds, became far better developed in the early nineteenth century. American natural history books had been written in the eighteenth century with such titles as *The American Grove* (1715), Mark Catesby's *Natural History* (1731), and William Bartram's *Travels* (1791). But a far more systematically inclusive American ornithology was created by a Scotsman who emigrated to America in 1794, Alexander Wilson. Influenced by Bartram, Wilson completed a series of drawings which were engraved by another Scottish immigrant in Philadelphia, Alexander Lawson. Published as a multi-volume series between 1808 and 1814, the work was internationally recognized as the definitive American ornithology until 1827, when Audubon's artistically triumphant *Birds of America* appeared.

James S. Glennie, watercolor, "A Sketch of the Forecastle and Main Deck of Thomas Penrose . . . ," in his manuscript journal, "The Particulars of and Sketches Taken During a Voyage to and Journey over the United States and Back, Commencing 24th September, 1810." Manuscripts. Gift of Andre de Coppet, Class of 1915. (*detail*)

· 1810 ·

James Glennie was a Scotsman and a pioneer artist-traveler who sailed on the ship *Thomas Penrose* on September 24, arriving in America on November 15, 1810. He painted several lively watercolors during the passage aboard the *Penrose*. After landing in Philadelphia, he travelled the Delaware River Road to Trenton, then to Princeton, New Brunswick, and New York which he found very much like a European city. He also toured the southern states and Washington, D.C., and met President Madison and his wife Dolley. He writes, "Mr. Madison appears to be a quiet man and in figure is quite diminutive, with an emaciated countenance. His lady is a jolly, sensible and pleasant woman. Considerably taller than her husband and what he wants in color she has."

The Glennie manuscript is full of the traveller's own watercolors and presents an incomparable recreation in word and image of life in America in 1810.

Jacob Bigelow, *American Medical Botany*. . . . Boston, 1817–1820. Rare Books. Gift of Sydnor B. Penick, Jr., Class of 1925.

· 1817 ·

The first American printed herbal and the first American book with color-printed plates is Bigelow's *American Medical Botany.* Since color is such an essential part of the description of plants, Bigelow was determined to present it as effectively as possible. Dissatisfied with hand-coloring, which was used for some of the first engraved plates for volume one, Bigelow's engravers, William Annin and George Smith, apparently turned to a color printing technique developed in France at this time, daubing colored inks *à la poupée* to the aquatint engraved copper to achieve strong color effects. A recent study of Bigelow's work, however, claims that the color plates are experiments in color lithography.* Since lithography in 1817 was still in its infancy, this idea seems beyond the technical capability of the period.

* Richard J. Wolfe, *Jacob Bigelow's American Medical Botany* (North Hills, Pennsylvania: Bird and Bull Press, 1979).

Bass Otis, unidentified scene, lithograph published in *The Analectic Magazine.* Philadelphia, 1819. Graphic Arts.

· 1819 ·

Usually accepted as the first lithography in America, this homely little drawing was executed on stone by Bass Otis. Aloys Senefelder patented this revolutionary new "chemical printing" technique in Munich in 1799. A drawing made by wax crayon or oil-based drawing-ink on Bavarian limestone will print its image, after the stone is moistened and inked, in an almost perfect facsimile. Thomas Dobson, the Philadelphia printer of the late eighteenth-century American *Encyclopaedia*, had presented a lithographic stone to the American Philosophical Society in Philadelphia, where Bass Otis was able to make this simple lithograph, the first known use in America of a process that would become a major graphic technique of the nineteenth century.

John Hill, colored aquatint engraving, title page from Joshua Shaw's *Picturesque Views of American Scenery.* Philadelphia, 1820. Graphic Arts. Gift of Leonard L. Milberg, Class of 1953.

· 1820 ·

New picture-printing techniques were very much in vogue in Philadelphia during the first decades of the nineteenth century. Lithography had been introduced by Bass Otis in Philadelphia in 1819, aquatint quickly followed in Joshua Shaw's portfolio of 1820, and the first Philadelphia daguerreotype, made by Joseph Saxton, introduced the photographic art to America in the same year as its discovery in France, 1839. Shaw's *Picturesque Views* were the first important aquatints of American scenery, and began a strong phase of American landscape rendering in the brilliant tonal technique of aquatint engraving.

John Hill, colored aquatint engraving after Joshua Shaw, "Passaic Falls, New Jersey," from Joshua Shaw's *Picturesque Views of American Scenery*. Philadelphia, 1820. Graphic Arts. Gift of Leonard L. Milberg, Class of 1953.

· 1820 ·

Both the new lithography and aquatint broke free of the pure line limitations of the woodcut and copper engraved prints seen in America up to this time. Aquatint engraving, developed in Europe in the eighteenth century, subjected the design on the copperplate to several successive etching "bites" in an acid bath, giving the image varying tonalities shade by shade, from the palest of grays to darkest black. The result is a lustrous tonality equal to the gradations of watercolor itself. Much favored in England, aquatint quickly found a new market in America through the masterful work of John Hill.

John Hill, hand-colored aquatint after William Guy Wall, "View near Hudson," number 15 of the *Hudson River Portfolio*. New York, 1820. Graphic Arts. Gift of Leonard L. Milberg, Class of 1953.

· 1820 ·

John Hill was one of several English engravers and artists who found a new home in America. Hill had learned the complexities of aquatint engraving in London before he arrived in this country in 1816. He engraved Shaw's *Picturesque Views* in Philadelphia in 1820 and immediately proceeded to create his masterpiece, *The Hudson River Portfolio*, which was issued in parts from 1820 to 1825. Hill sent for his family in 1819 and settled in New York City from 1822 to 1836. He was the father of the important landscape painter John William Hill and grandfather of landscape painter and etcher John Henry Hill.

Axel Klinckowstrom, *Brodway-gatan och Radhuseti Newyork* (Broadway and City Hall in New York). Stockholm, 1824. Rare Books. Gift of Erik Sjöqvist.

· 1824 ·

The international spread of aquatint as a print medium is seen in Sweden as early as 1824. Axel Klinckowstrom visited America in 1819, and in his travels painted a number of beautifully observed watercolors of the American scene. Returning to Sweden, he had many of them published in aquatint engravings, including this early view of Broadway and City Hall. Despite the elegance of the scene, pigs are still seen running free along the street.

Titian Ramsay Peale, colored engraving for Thomas Say, *American Entomology, or Descriptions of the Insects of North America*, 3 volumes. Philadelphia, 1824–1828. Rare Books.

· 1824 ·

American art and science merged in natural-history book illustration of the 1820s, when two classics of American natural science appeared: Thomas Say's *American Entomology* in 1824, and John James Audubon's great *Birds of America* in 1827. Say was curator of the American Philosophical Society and Academy of Natural Sciences of Philadelphia, professor of natural history in the University of Pennsylvania, and of zoology in the Philadelphia Museum. The Charles Willson Peale family also joined art and science, opening to the public its famous and successful Peale Museum of Natural History, and one of the sons, Titian Peale, did many illustrations for Say's *Entomology.*

John James Audubon, pen and watercolor drawing, "Yellow-Throated Vireo." Signed and dated 1827. Graphic Arts, Iconography Collection. Gift of John S. Williams, Class of 1924.

· 1827 ·

One of the greatest of all color plate books, *The Birds of America*, was the result of creative collaboration between its American artist, John James Audubon, and its skilled English engraver, Robert Havell, Jr. Rarely have artistic imagination, scientific observation, and technical execution been better wed in one grand enterprise. Published in an elephant folio edition to maintain the life-size scale of all birds, the work was issued in parts between 1827 and 1838, and far surpassed the earlier relatively awkward ornithological plates of Alexander Wilson. It is the American illustrated book now most celebrated by critical and popular esteem throughout the world, due in part to widespread reproduction of its superlative aquatint engravings and several later editions in smaller format.

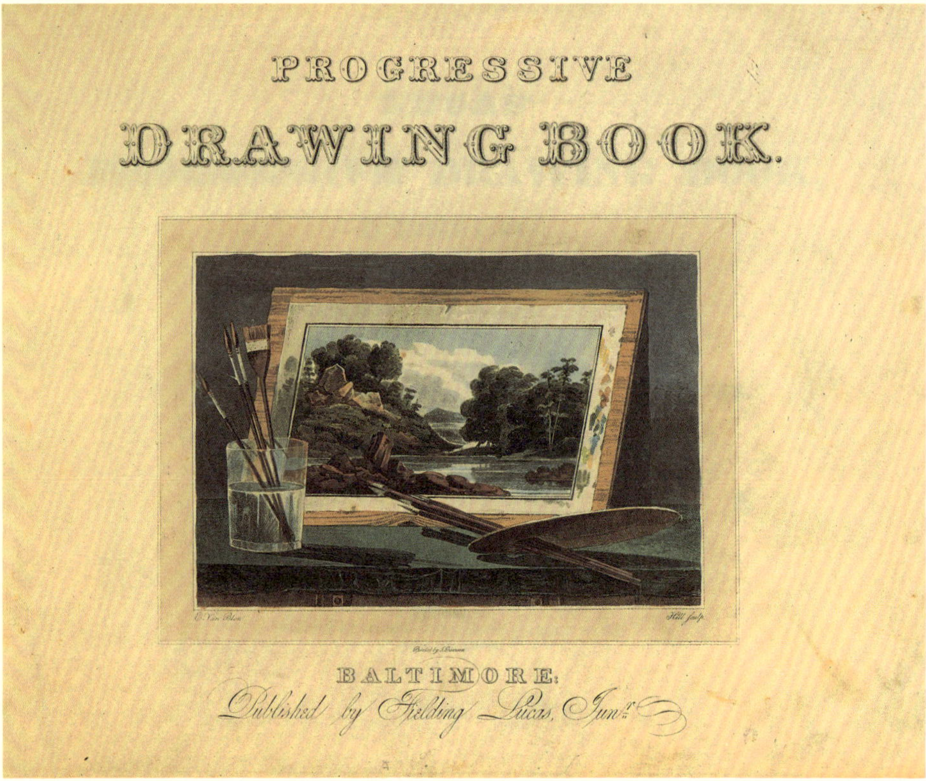

John Hill, engraving after John Hazlehurst Boneval Latrobe, *Progressive Drawing Book*. Baltimore, 1827. Graphic Arts. Gift of Leonard L. Milberg, Class of 1953.

· 1827 ·

The great aquatint color-plate books of the 1820s, including such masterworks as the *Hudson River Portfolio* and the *Birds of America*, led inevitably to a strongly increased cultural awareness not only of American flora and fauna, but also of American scenery as a proper and patriotic subject for students and amateurs of art. The first important American manual on how to draw and watercolor landscapes was published in 1827. The plates were engraved in aquatint by John Hill after the drawings of John Latrobe, who was the son of Washington architect Benjamin Latrobe. The young Latrobe also journeyed through the South to create a beautiful series of small watercolors as a travel diary.

Zuber et Cie., color wood-blocked wall paper fragment showing Boston, one of a series of panels depicting the cities of America. Paris, ca. 1830. Gift of Leonard L. Milberg, Class of 1953.

· ca. 1830 ·

Scenic wallpapers became the height of fashion in the Federal period. Imported from France, *papier-peint* mural scenes, printed by hand from woodcut blocks in many colors, were to be seen in affluent American homes from Virginia to New England. A fine example is the "Monuments of Paris" pattern, originally presented by Dufour of Paris in 1815; it may be seen on the walls of the Richmond Room in the Metropolitan Museum of Art, New York. In the same cosmopolitan fashion, another Parisian firm, Zuber et Cie., published a series called "American Scenery" that must have included this pastoral view of Boston.

Jacques-Gerard Milbert, lithograph, "Vue de New-York prise de Weahawk (A view of New York taken from Weehawken, New Jersey)," in his *Itinéraire pittoresque du Fleuve Hudson.* Paris, 1828–1829. Graphic Arts. Gift of Leonard L. Milberg, Class of 1953.

· 1828 ·

Jacques-Gerard Milbert was a remarkable French scholar, engineer, and artist who came to the United States in 1815 and remained for eight years. His fascination with American natural history led him to collect more than 7,000 American shells, plants, feathers, and minerals which are now in the Museum of Natural History in Paris. He also was a masterful draftsman, and fifty-four of his American drawings were issued in lithographs in the folio volume *Itinéraire pittoresque du Fleuve Hudson.* The book is a rare French vision of America, printed in Paris with the advanced skill of French lithographers of this period.

Ambrose Louis Garneray, aquatint engraving, *Vue de New York*. Paris, ca. 1829. Lent by Leonard L. Milberg, Class of 1953.

· ca. 1829 ·

Another fine French vision of nineteenth-century America may be seen in the aquatint scenery of Ambrose Garneray. Although Garneray never came to America, he made several splendid aquatint views of American ports, including Baltimore, Boston, New York, New Orleans, and Philadelphia. He must have seen and copied the Milbert lithograph to compose his view of New York from Weehawken. The serene landscape offers almost unbelievable contrast to present day Manhattan. Near where the couple ambles by is now the gaping entrance to the roaring Holland Tunnel; where church spires catch the sun are now the shadowed canyons of Wall Street and the World Trade Center.

John Hill, aquatint engraving after William James Bennett, *Niagara Falls. Part of the American Fall from the Foot of the Stair Case.* New York, 1829–1830. Graphic Arts. Gift of Leonard L. Milberg, Class of 1953.

· 1829–1830 ·

The English artist and engraver William James Bennett arrived in New York in 1824, where he met Henry J. Megarey. Under Megarey's enterprising patronage, Bennett published his first American aquatints of New York City street-scenes. In 1829 Bennett travelled to Niagara Falls, where he painted for Megarey two views of the falls. These early Bennett prints began a long series of American views unequalled for their romantic vision since the *Hudson River Portfolio*.

In addition to the pair of Hill-Bennett views, Bennett himself engraved two other views of Niagara Falls in 1830, both taken from Goat Island. The brilliance of these two later landscapes must have helped his election to the American Academy of De-

John Hill, aquatint engraving after William James Bennett, *Niagara Falls, Part of the British Fall Taken from Under the Table Rock.* New York, 1829–1830. Graphic Arts. Gift of Leonard L. Milberg, Class of 1953.

sign, which had just been established in 1829 as America's answer to Great Britain's Royal Academy. The Niagara Falls prints also elicited the admiration of the *New York Mirror* critic, who wrote on May 14, 1831, "We have seldom met among the numerous delineations of this stupendous wonder more forcible impression . . . everything but the deafening thunder [is] represented to the life. . . ."* One of Bennett's Niagara prints even inspired imitation in a painted laquer binding design for an elaborate "gift book," *The Philopoena.*

* Gloria-Gilda Deák, *William James Bennett, Master of the Aquatint View* (New York, 1988).

"Blue Crane, Hudsonian Godwit," *The Cabinet of Natural History and Rural Sports*, 2 volumes. Philadelphia, 1830–1832. Rare Books.
Gift of Carl Otto von Kienbusch, Class of 1906.

· 1832 ·

Thomas Doughty, who would become one of the leaders of the Hudson River School of landscape painting, published with his brother John this first color-illustrated sporting book about America. Many of the lithographs are signed as the work of Cephas G. Childs, who helped pioneer the first important lithographic printing firm in Philadelphia, Pendleton, Kearny and Childs. Cephas Childs was the driving force of the firm, which soon gave Philadelphia the lead in the emerging graphic arts industry of lithography.* Albert Newsam, a highly gifted deaf mute who became one of Philadelphia's best lithographers, was Childs' student, and Peter Duval, who helped pioneer color lithography, was Childs' later partner.

* Nicholas B. Wainwright, *Philadelphia in the Romantic Age of Lithography* (Philadelphia, 1958).

John Hill, colored aquatint after Thomas Doughty, *Fair Mount Water Works.* Philadelphia, 1832. Graphic Arts. Gift of Leonard L. Milberg, Class of 1953.

· 1832 ·

Designed by William Strickland, the Philadelphia waterworks is a fine example of classic revival architecture, deftly combining the picturesque with the practical. Doughty was one of many artists to paint this charming cluster of classical temples on the Schuylkill River. Doughty's landscapes are early examples of American local scenery suffused with the landscape tradition of Claude Lorraine. It was a stylistic ideal that would later lead to the work of fellow Hudson River painters Thomas Cole and Asher Durand.

Karl Bodmer, "Missouri Indian, Oto Indian, Chief of the Puncas," from Maximilian, Prince von Wied-Neuwied, *Travels in the Interior of North America, 1832–1834*. London, 1839–1844. Princeton Collections of Western Americana. Gift of Philip Ashton Rollins, Class of 1889.

· 1832 ·

Karl Bodmer was a Swiss artist and engraver who accompanied Maximilian, Prince von Wied-Neuwied, on an exploratory expedition to the United States in the years 1832–1834. Bodmer had an extraordinary eye for the scenery and Indians of the still existing wilds of America, and created hundreds of beautifully observed watercolors and drawings. Eighty-one of these were engraved in aquatint and printed as the plates of Maximilian's *Travels in the Interior of North America, 1832–1834*, which appeared in print from 1839 to 1844. Matching the high quality of Bodmer's watercolors was a problem, and a few, now very rare, copies, including the one at Princeton, were printed experimentally in colored inks.

Charles Vogel, engraved aquatint after Karl Bodmer, "View on the Delaware Near Bordentown," leaf from Maximilian, Prince von Wied-Neuwied, *Travels in the Interior of North America*. . . . London, 1832–1839. Graphic Arts.

· 1832 ·

Rudolf Ackermann, the London publisher of the Maximilian *Travels*, turned to full hand-coloring of the Bodmer plates for better effect. One of the vignettes was an engraved aquatint by Charles Vogel after Bodmer showing the Bordentown, New Jersey, garden of Joseph Bonaparte, Napoleon's elder brother. The Maximilian-Bodmer *Travels*, like Audubon's *Birds of America*, is among the finest color-plate books ever published, and a splendid example of the collaborative efforts of artist, engraver, colorist, and printer.

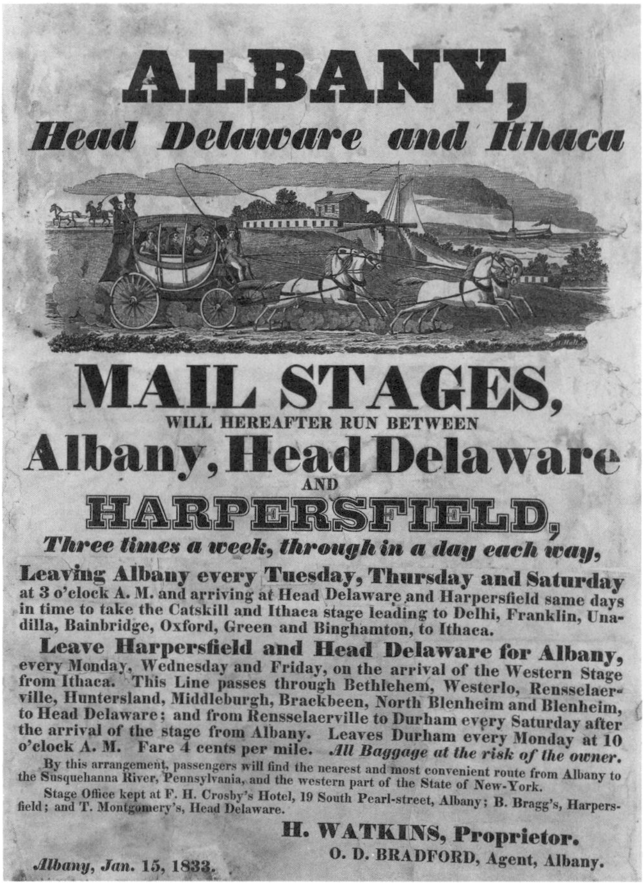

ALBANY,
Head Delaware and Ithaca

MAIL STAGES,
WILL HEREAFTER RUN BETWEEN
Albany, Head Delaware
AND
HARPERSFIELD,
Three times a week, through in a day each way,

Leaving Albany every Tuesday, Thursday and Saturday at 3 o'clock A. M. and arriving at Head Delaware and Harpersfield same days in time to take the Catskill and Ithaca stage leading to Delhi, Franklin, Unadilla, Bainbridge, Oxford, Green and Binghamton, to Ithaca.

Leave Harpersfield and Head Delaware for Albany, every Monday, Wednesday and Friday, on the arrival of the Western Stage from Ithaca. This Line passes through Bethlehem, Westerlo, Rensselaerville, Huntersland, Middleburgh, Brackbeen, North Blenheim and Blenheim, to Head Delaware; and from Rensselaerville to Durham every Saturday after the arrival of the stage from Albany. Leaves Durham every Monday at 10 o'clock A. M. Fare 4 cents per mile. *All Baggage at the risk of the owner.*

By this arrangement, passengers will find the nearest and most convenient route from Albany to the Susquehanna River, Pennsylvania, and the western part of the State of New-York.

Stage Office kept at F. H. Crosby's Hotel, 19 South Pearl-street, Albany; B. Bragg's, Harpersfield; and T. Montgomery's, Head Delaware.

H. WATKINS, Proprietor.
O. D. BRADFORD, Agent, Albany.

Albany, Jan. 15, 1833.

John H. Hall after John A. Woodside, Jr. wood engraved broadside, *Albany, Head Delaware and Ithaca Mail Stages*. . . . Albany, 1833. Graphic Arts. The Sinclair Hamilton Collection.

· 1833 ·

Transportation in America was still primitive in the 1830s, but a growing sense of excitement in travel may be seen in such boldly printed broadsides as this early poster, with its flying horses and elegant coach. The new Erie Canal, with canal boat and canal lock, may be seen in the background. The bold typefaces are the latest word in English typographic fashion, and were increasingly imported for early American advertising. Carved in wood, such typefaces became progressively more over-weighted and over-embellished with each passing decade until their riotous climax in Victorian circus posters of the 1880s.

Abel Bowen, woodcut broadside, *For Albany . . . Steamboat Fanny.* New York, 1834. Graphic Arts. The Sinclair Hamilton Collection.

· 1834 ·

Vigorous woodcut broadsides announced time and place of departure of boats and included some of the best wood-engraved images of the period. Abel Bowen was particularly adept at proud, graphically energized cuts of ships in full sail or puffing steam. He was also a prolific book illustrator. There are some twenty-seven of his books in the Sinclair Hamilton Collection at Princeton. Travel in these years included not only steamboat and stage coach, but also the beginning of the railroad. The first successful run of an American steam locomotive was made in August of 1830 aboard Peter Cooper's "Tom Thumb."

Asher B. Durand, engraving after Samuel F.B. Morse, "Evening at Home," for *Godey's Lady's Book*. New York, 1834. Graphic Arts.

· 1834 ·

Born and raised in New Jersey, Asher Durand became one of the great painters of the Hudson River School of landscape painting. Early in his remarkable career this New Jersey native left the farm to be apprenticed to the engraving trade in New York. By age twenty-four Durand was among the most successful producers of banknote vignettes and special plates for the new "gift book annuals," the two uses of copperplate engraving most in demand. The "annuals" were first imported to America from England in 1824 and prospered through most of the century as fancy purveyors of culture combined with sentiment.

Asher B. Durand, engraving after John Vanderlyn, *Ariadne*. New York, 1835. The Art Museum, Princeton University.

· 1835 ·

Durand soon became the leading engraver on copper of the day, and was responsible for significant innovations both technical and aesthetic. He replaced copper with steel for the printing plate, and introduced the now familiar iconography of allegorical nudes into bank note engraving. Related to this early use of engraved nudes is Durand's surprising purchase of the most celebrated early American painting of a nude, John Vanderlyn's *Ariadne*. Durand proceeded to make his own masterful engraved reproduction, which James Flexner finds more aesthetically complete than the Vanderlyn original.* It is by far the most ambitious and beautifully realized pure line engraving by an American up to this time.

* James Flexner, *History of American Painting*, 3 vols. (New York, 1962); Vol. 3: *That Wilder Image, The Native School from Thomas Cole to Winslow Homer*, pp. 54–56.

John T. Bowen after Charles Bird King, color lithograph, "Se-Quo-Yah," in Thomas Lorraine McKenney and James Hall, *History of the Indian Tribes of North America. . . .* Philadelphia, 1836–1838. Rare Books. Gift of Jasper E. Crane, Class of 1901.

· 1836–1838 ·

Charles Bird King began his career as a portrait painter, and studied, like all the best Americans, with Benjamin West in London. Returning to America, he began a series of formal portraits of Indians. His Indian Gallery in Philadelphia caught the interest of a publisher, Frederick Greenough, who hired lithographers George Lehman and Peter Duval to transfer King's paintings to stone. In 1838, another lithographer, John T. Bowen, was brought in to complete the work. Bowen's lithograph of Se-Quo-Yah is especially interesting because it shows an educated and civilized Indian who invented a written Cherokee alphabet. He wears the peace medal given him by the President. Since most of King's original paintings were destroyed by fire at the Smithsonian in 1865, these lithographs are an invaluable record of a noble American race as they were in the 1830s.

Peter Duval after Charles Bird King, color lithograph, "Ki-On-Twog-Ky," in Thomas Lorraine McKenney and James Hall, *History of the Indian Tribes of North America.* Philadelphia, 1838–1844. Rare Books. Gift of Mrs. Edgar Palmer.

· 1838–1844 ·

The series of color lithographs of Indians, begun by George Lehman and Peter Duval, was completed by an outstanding colorist and lithographer, John T. Bowen, who moved from New York to Philadelphia in 1838 to work on the project. The *History of the Indian Tribes* series established Bowen's reputation as the best printmaker in the nation, and the completed volumes were hailed as "one of the largest and most splendid works which the literature and arts of the country has ever produced."*

* *Saturday Courier,* Philadelphia, 24 November 1838.

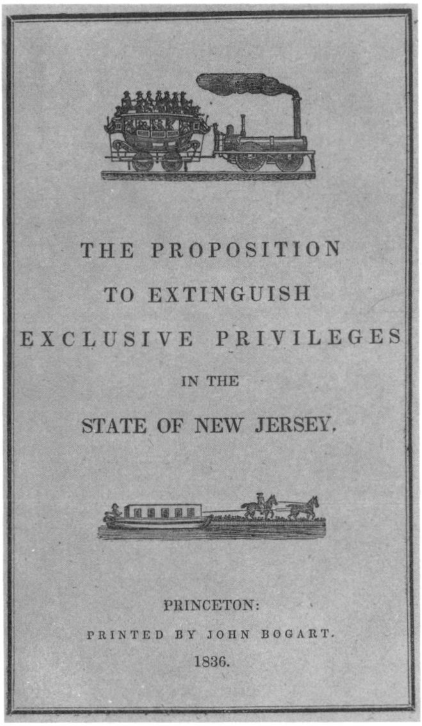

John Bogart, pamphlet, *The Proposition to Extinguish Exclusive Privileges in the State of New Jersey.* Princeton, 1836. Graphic Arts. The Sinclair Hamilton Collection.

· 1836 ·

Halfway between New York and Philadelphia, Princeton always enjoyed a position as a main stop for the stage coach as well as the canal boat and the railroad. Completion of the Delaware and Raritan canal in 1834 meant great changes in New Jersey, and was the precursor of ever faster transport in this part of the country. The railroad soon followed. This 1836 Princeton imprint by John Bogart shows wood-engraved vignettes of both the horse-drawn canal boat and the early steam engine. The "Daedalus" engine was soon pulling stage-coach shaped cars at seemingly breathtaking speed through New Brunswick, Princeton, and Trenton. The same juxtaposition of canal and train is seen in Augustus Köllner's later watercolor of the Delaware River (see 1844).

Joseph Alexander Adams after William Sidney Mount, frontispiece for volume two of William Dunlap, *A History of New York for Schools*, two volumes in one. New York, 1837. Graphic Arts, The Sinclair Hamilton Collection.

· 1837 ·

This modest little book is by William Dunlap, author of the first important history of American art.* In this 1837 history of New York, Dunlap was able to obtain illustrations by two of the best artists of the day. Based on the designs of William Sidney Mount, one of the most original of all painters of the American scene, the engraver Joseph Alexander Adams created for Dunlap illustrations technically surpassing most work done to this date in wood. Adams' handling of pure line to express the chiaroscuro of full light and shade in this rural image is a small tour de force, predating similar effects in the much later prints after Winslow Homer.

* William Dunlap, *The History of the Rise and Progress of the Arts of Design in the United States* (New York, 1834).

David Claypoole Johnston, watercolor drawing with a concealed message: "D. C. Johnston, Teacher of Landscape Drawing and Painting." Boston, 1837. Graphic Arts. Gift of Leonard L. Milberg, Class of 1953.

· 1837 ·

Trained as an actor, Johnston turned from a career on the stage to become one of the most popular illustrators of his time. He was fond of graphic tricks, and made several caricature "metamorphoses" cards that changed in delightfully upstart ways to ridicule political and social figures of the day. He called himself "Strait Shanks" and became well-known as the "American Cruikshank." He was fully as versatile, if not as prolific, as his English counterpart, George Cruikshank, and worked equally well in watercolor, lithography, etching and wood engraving.

Alexander Jackson Davis, color lithograph, "A Residence in the English Collegiate Style," *Rural Residences*. . . . New York, 1837. Graphic Arts, The Sinclair Hamilton Collection.

· 1837 ·

Alexander Jackson Davis is mainly remembered as a dominant early force in American architecture, but he began his career as a draftsman and lithographer. His *Rural Residences* of 1837 presents prospective clients with drawings of his house designs, most of them humbly set in the American landscape. His "Residence in the English Collegiate Style," however, is more evocative of early medieval English castles and presents a strong new taste for Gothic revival in America. *Rural Residences* is printed with both early John Pendleton lithography and a fine cover vignette, also of a Gothic villa, by Samuel F.B. Morse.

3

Joseph's erster Traum.

Jakob hatte zwölf Söhne, von welchen die zwölf Stämme der Kinder Israel herstammen. Unter allen diesen Söhnen war keiner welcher die Liebe seines Vaters mehr verdiente, als Joseph. Deswegen aber haßten ihn seine Brüder, und konnten es nicht ertragen, ihn mit einem bunten Rocke bekleidet zu sehen, welchen ihm sein Vater hatte machen lassen. Als Joseph siebenzehn Jahre alt war, da träumte er, daß seine Brüder und er Garben auf dem Felde bänden, und daß seine Garbe aufstand, und die übrigen

4

Joseph's zweiter Traum.

sich alle vor ihr neigten. Ein anderes Mal träumte ihm, daß die Sonne, der Mond und eilf Sterne sich vor ihm neigten. Als das seinem Vater gesagt ward, so strafte er ihn, und sprach: "Was ist das für ein Traum, soll ich und deine Mutter und deine Brüder kommen und dich anbeten? Bald darauf wurde Joseph von seinem Vater hinaus aufs Feld geschickt, um zu sehen, was seine Brüder machen, wie ihn diese kommen sahen, sprachen sie: Sehet, der Träumer kommt daher, lasset uns ihn erwürgen, und in eine Grube wer-

Gustave Peters, *Die Geschichte Joseph's und seiner Brüder.* Harrisburg, Pennsylvania, 1837. Graphic Arts, The Sinclair Hamilton Collection.

· 1837 ·

Similar to Jonathan Fisher in Blue Hill, Maine, for its naive but inspired work, the print shop of Gustave Peters in Harrisburg, Pennsylvania, was a remarkable outpost of early American printing on the handpress. This German immigrant printer created as early as 1826 several impeccable little books for German-speaking children that contain woodcut pictures printed entirely in color. Gustave Peters is the earliest known color printer of such pictures in America.*

* Kirke Bryan, *The First American Color Printer* (Norristown, Pennsylvania, 1957).

Henry Walton, *View of Ithaca, New York, Taken from West Hill.* New York, 1839. Graphic Arts. Gift of Leonard L. Milberg, Class of 1953. (*detail*)

· 1839 ·

Henry Walton set up his studio in Ithaca, in upstate New York, in 1839. In this same year he drew on a lithographic stone a truly affectionate panoramic vista of the still rural community as it was about twenty-five years before Cornell University was founded. In this very finely colored and meticulously detailed image, Walton achieved a degree of lithographic rendering and overall freshness of vision that elevates the print beyond topographical record to a beautifully realized work of art.

John Warner Barber, *A History of the Amistad Captives*. . . . New Haven, 1840. Graphic Arts, The Sinclair Hamilton Collection.

· 1840 ·

Certain wood engravers of the nineteenth century seem indefatigable. One was Alexander Anderson, "the father of American wood engraving"; another was John Warner Barber, nicknamed "the picture preacher." Among hundreds of books illustrated by Barber, well described by Sinclair Hamilton as "earnest but uninspired," at least one stands out for inspiring his passion. This book is an account of the rebellion on the slave ship *Amistad* in 1839, and the subsequent capture and trial of the slaves and their leader, Cinque, in New Haven. Barber's lurid picture of the uprising subtly contradicts the more fair-minded text defending the mutiny.

William Henry Bartlett, color engraving, "New Haven Green," from N. P. Willis, *American Scenery*. London, 1840. Graphic Arts, The Sinclair Hamilton Collection.

· 1840 ·

English artist William Bartlett made four visits to the United States, touring the country to make his carefully detailed drawings that would be engraved for a popular illustrated travel guide, N. P. Willis' *American Scenery*. Wilderness is supplanted by the picturesque, and there is more English pastoral imagery to these pictures than recognizable American terrain. It is an example of a newly popular genre, the "annual gift book," prettily hand-colored and bound up in a heavy gilt and ornamented binding. The Bartlett views present an anglicized vision of the American scene very different from the rugged woodcuts of John Warner Barber.

William James Bennett, aquatint engraving after George Harvey, "A Road Accident," from *Harvey's Scenes of the Primitive Forest of America*. New York, 1841. Lent by Leonard L. Milberg, Class of 1953.

· 1841 ·

George Harvey came to America from England as an already well established watercolor painter. At his new home in Hastings-on-Hudson he was a neighbor of Washington Irving, and he designed for him the charming house on the Hudson that became known as "Sunnyside." Harvey was fascinated by the changing effects of light on the American landscape, both during the day and through the seasons. He painted some forty of his inimitable water colors, which he planned to publish as *Harvey's American Scenery*, showing the atmospheric and lighting changes he observed throughout the year. Sadly, financial problems thwarted the project, and only four paintings, one for each season, were engraved in aquatint by William James Bennett and published in portfolio in 1841.

John James Audubon, watercolor, *Striped Ground Squirrel (Say's Chipmunk)*. Place unknown, 1841. Graphic Arts, Iconography Collection. Gift of John S. Williams, Class of 1924.

· 1841 ·

The triumph of John James Audubon's *Birds of America* led inevitably to the idea of another great American natural history book about the animals of North America. From about 1839 Audubon was assisted by the American naturalist, John Bachman, and eventually by his own sons John and Victor, in this new project. He also had an American lithographer, John T. Bowen (see 1836–1838), to draw the plates on stone. *The Viviparous Quadrupeds of North America* (1845–1854) was produced in Philadelphia, rather than in England, thus creating a far more truly American production than *Birds of America* had been. Princeton's extensive Audubon holdings include two fine watercolor studies of the striped ground squirrel that were combined for Plate 24 of the *Quadrupeds*.

Alfred M. Hoffy, *The Orchardist's Companion, A Quarterly Journal*. Philadelphia, 1841. Rare Books. (*detail*)

· 1841 ·

The illustration of North America naturally embraced not only scenery and indigenous species of plants and animals, but also the products of the land. One of the first of many illustrated works devoted to American fruits and flowers was the *Orchardist's Companion*, "embellished with richly colored designs of the natural size, painted from the actual fruits when in their finest condition." The lithographer of the ripely rendered plates was Alfred Hoffy, who worked in Philadelphia until after 1860, when he published his definitive apple book, *The North American Pomologist*. Both these works were examples of a whole new genre of nurserymen's and gardeners' seed catalogues illustrated with American produce.

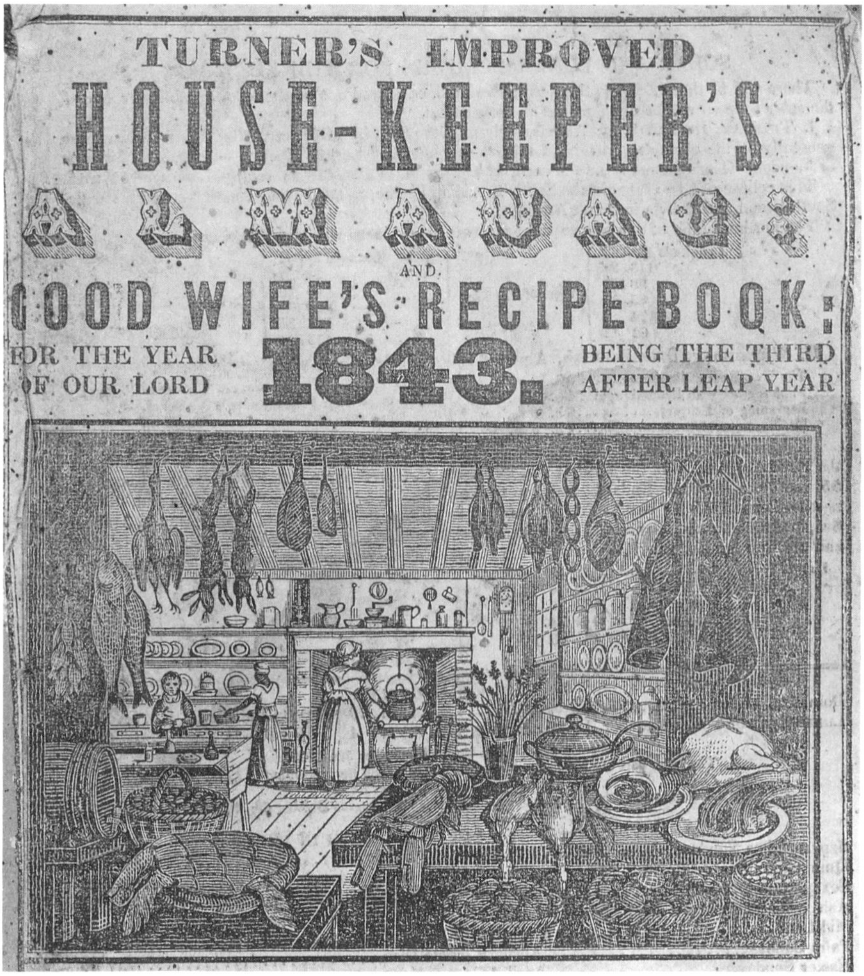

Turner's Improved House-Keeper's Almanac: Good Wife's Recipe Book. Philadelphia, 1843. Graphic Arts, The Sinclair Hamilton Collection.

· 1843 ·

Cookbooks are a good indicator of a civilized society, and America had many of these essential books for the kitchen. The first was published as early as 1796, and many almanacs for the following years of the nineteenth century included household and cooking wisdom. This 1843 housekeeper's almanac is full of perennial good advice, and has as cover a woodcut of a bountiful, larder-laden kitchen.

Alfred Jacob Miller, watercolor, *Indian Guide*. Baltimore, Maryland, ca. 1840–1842. Princeton Collections of Western Americana. Gift of Mrs. Laurence R. Carton and William Pinkney Carton, Class of 1943.

· ca. 1842 ·

While travelling with Captain William Drummond Stewart on an expedition into the Rocky Mountains, Alfred Jacob Miller was able to create about a hundred watercolor sketches of Indian life. The leader of the expedition, Captain Stewart, is portrayed here on his white horse, communicating in sign language to an Indian guide. Sketched originally from direct observation, Miller later redrew and elaborated the drawings in his Baltimore studio from 1840–1842. Such studio reworking of his on-the-spot sketches may account for the idyllic, somewhat romantic cast of Miller's best-known work.

George Catlin, colored lithograph, "A Visit to Washington," from *Catlin's North American Indian Portfolio*. London, 1844. The Scheide Library.

· 1844 ·

Portrayals of the American Indian from Theodore de Bry to Alfred Jacob Miller continued to display a romantic image that was difficult to dispel. Karl Bodmer (1832) and Charles Bird King (1836) had presented Indian faces with far greater truth, but George Catlin now injected an almost harsh realism into his drawings and lithographs. Travelling to the West in 1830, he began his lifetime occupation of painting the Indians and their already vanishing customs. By 1844, he published his *North American Indian Portfolio*, drawing with some bitterness the easy corrupting influence of liquor and white men's ways on an Indian chief after a visit to Washington.

Frederick Catherwood, self-portrait with John L. Stephens, in his colored lithograph, "The Ruins of Tulum," (Mexico), from Catherwood's *Views of Ancient Monuments*. London, 1844. Lent by Leonard L. Milberg, Class of 1953. (*detail*)

· 1844 ·

By the 1840s artists in Europe had found far more historically significant uses for lithography. Following the aquatint travel-book tradition, a series of landmark travel and discovery folios illustrated by lithography were published in London, among them this monumental pictorial work on ancient American ruins in Mexico, Frederick Catherwood's *Views of Ancient Monuments*. This great work represents Catherwood's brilliantly expanded illustration of John L. Stephen's two-volume *Incidents of Travel in Central America, Chiapas and the Yucatan*, and includes his personally colored lithographs of the drawings and watercolors he made on the journey with Stephens in the autumn of 1841. By 1844 Catherwood published a folio volume of his beautifully detailed lithographs, which have become a fundamental source for the study of Mayan civilization.

Nathaniel Currier, colored lithograph, *Awful Explosion of the "Peace-Maker" on Board the U.S. Steam Frigate*, Princeton, *on Wednesday,* 28*th Feby.* 1844. New York, 1844. Graphic Arts. (*detail*)

· 1844 ·

The illustration of news events soon became an essential role of the lithographer. Young Nathaniel Currier issued within weeks his prints of the USS *Princeton* and the disastrous explosion of Commander Robert Stockton's newly designed cannon, the "Peace-Maker," during its inspection by President Tyler and his cabinet. Many men were killed, including members of the cabinet, but Tyler escaped injury. Currier joined forces in 1857 with another lithographer, James M. Ives. Together they would create a new print industry combining pictorial journalism and popular imagery in "prints for the people."

John Warner Barber, "College of New Jersey, Princeton," in John Warner Barber and Henry Howe, *Historical Collections of the State of New Jersey.* New York, 1844. Graphic Arts, The Sinclair Hamilton Collection.

· 1844 ·

Among the many ambitious projects of John Warner Barber were his "Historical Collections" which included his wood-engraved illustrations and written history of nearly every town in Connecticut (1836), Massachusetts (1839), New York (1841), New Jersey (1844), and Virginia (1845). Dressed in top hat and cape, Barber travelled through New England and Virginia, patiently sketching local townships as he went. Tolerated as a character and antiquarian, he became known as the "picture preacher," and was legendary as chronicler of his time and place (see 1839).

Augustus Köllner, watercolor, *Washington's Crossing on the Delaware River.* Washington's Crossing, New Jersey, 1844. Graphic Arts.

· 1844 ·

Augustus Köllner was a German immigrant artist who, like John Warner Barber, travelled the country making highly picturesque drawings and watercolors. He journeyed up the Delaware in 1844, stopping at Washington's Crossing to make this pastoral landscape enlivened with both canal boat and early railroad. Köllner was very active, and in addition to his hundreds of drawings, he published fifty-four lithographic views of American cities from 1848 to 1851.

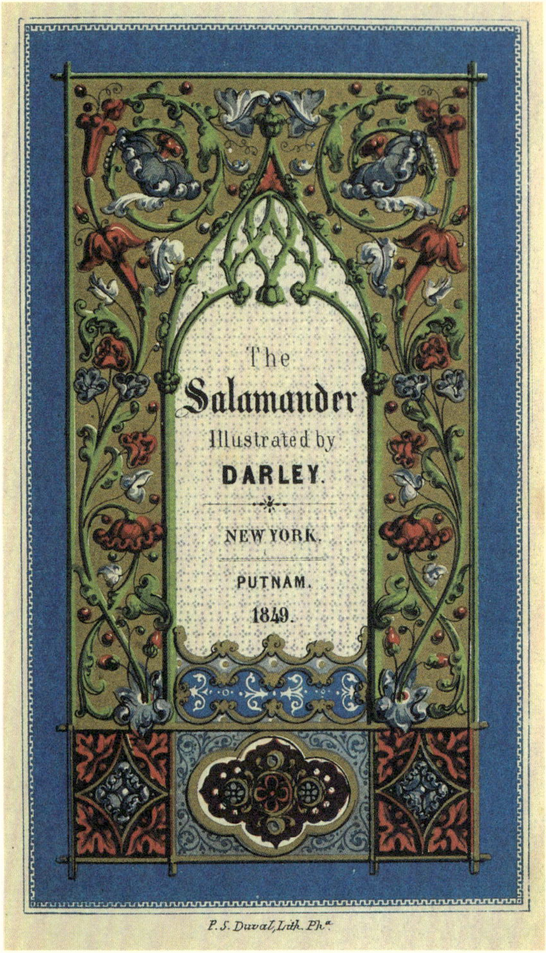

Peter Duval, color-printed lithograph half-title page (New York, 1849) for *The Salamander: A Legend for Christmas*. Philadelphia, 1848.
Graphic Arts.

· 1849 ·

Peter Duval has been introduced as a lithographer of the Charles Bird King Indian atlas of 1838, but his chief claim to fame in American graphic arts is his pioneering work in full-color lithography. By 1849 he had mastered the problems of colored inks and registry to produce such miniature jewels of color printing as this "illuminated" title. The idea of medieval illumination is closely associated with early color work as part of the American Gothic

Herline and Co., color lithograph advertisement for C. J. Fell and Brother. Philadelphia, no date. Graphic Arts.

revival, and early color lithographers worked in something of the same spirit as medieval illuminators. Both Duval's work and similar color prints of the 1840s and 1850s were able to adopt with startling success two of the most difficult-to-match colors of medieval pigments, azure blue and gold. Less medieval in intent is the simultaneous emergence of color in advertising, an idea that would proliferate beyond all imagination in later decades (see 1882).

William Howland, wood engraving, "American Art Union," in George C. Foster, *New York in Slices: by an Experienced Carver.* New York, 1849. Graphic Arts, The Sinclair Hamilton Collection.

· 1849 ·

From 1841 to 1847 the number of subscribers to the American Art Union, a cultural enterprise devoted to the support of the work of living American artists, increased from 814 to 9,666. The organization, which operated as a beneficent lottery, did much to promote American art. It distributed with great success engraved prints after the best artists of the day, including Frederick Church, John F. Kensett, Jasper Cropsey, John Doughty, and many others. The *New York in Slices* article on the American Art Union ends with some cultural smugness: "[We are] fearless of being accused of partiality by any who rightly appreciate the influences of the fine arts upon the morals and refinement of mankind."

William Howland, engraving, "View from the American Museum," in George C. Foster, *New York in Slices. . . .* New York, 1849. Graphic Arts, The Sinclair Hamilton Collection.

· 1849 ·

At the same time that itinerant artists such as John Warner Barber and Augustus Köllner were recording the small towns and countryside, New York City was beginning to stir as the great American cultural metropolis. This 1849 book records some of the rising problems of the big city, but it also describes the beginnings of big-city amenities. Brady's "Gallery of Daguerrotypes" is pictured at 205 Broadway, "Dag'd" by Brady, engraved by William Howland. Art, music, and the theatre are all described in the text as well-established in New York and beginning to flourish.

Carl Nebel, color lithograph, "Genl. Scott's Entrance into Mexico," from George Wilkins Kendall, *The War between the United States and Mexico Illustrated. . . .* New York and Philadelphia, 1851. Rare Books.

· 1850–1851 ·

The annexation of Texas precipitated war between Mexico and the United States in December 1845. By 1847 General Winfield Scott entered Mexico City. The battles of the Mexican-American War were painted by Carl Nebel and lithographed in Paris by the premier international lithographic firm of Lemercier. Like the Milbert folio of 1828 this ambitious color-plate book shows American history and scenery through French eyes and French printing. The preface belabors the effort and the expense involved: "They have certainly bestowed much time and money on the undertaking and [the author] can boldly assert that no country can claim that its battles have been illustrated in a richer, more faithful or more costly style of lithography."

Alfred Jones, colored engraving after the painting by Richard Caton Woodville, *Mexican News*. New York, 1851. Graphic Arts. Gift of Leonard L. Milberg, Class of 1953.

· 1851 ·

Among the best-received engravings distributed by the American Art Union was the Richard Caton Woodville, *Mexican News*, which illustrates the lively reaction at home to news from the Mexican-American War. Woodville is a particularly good example of American *genre* painters who studied in the German studios at Düsseldorf during these years. He sent many of his beautifully realistic paintings to America, and was a favorite of the American Art Union. Their engraving of *Mexican News* was even advertised in a miniature version, a print-selling idea used by Hogarth a century earlier.

Louis Rosenthal, chromolithograph, "Woodpecker," in Henry L. Stephens, *The Comic Natural History of the Human Race*. Philadelphia, 1851. Graphic Arts, The Sinclair Hamilton Collection.

· 1851–1852 ·

Wood engraving for books became a major trade by the mid-nineteenth century, and as a way of printing pictures the technique flourished through the century. This amazing book of caricatures of various Philadelphia celebrities in 1851 even includes a wood engraver, William B. Gihon, as "Woodpecker." It is printed not by wood, however, but in the chromolithography of a Philadelphia pioneer in color printing, Louis Rosenthal. He was among the first of a number of adventurous craftsmen to develop in Philadelphia a little recognized but historically significant school of color printing. Peter Duval led the way, followed by such rival workers in the emerging art as Thomas Sinclair, the firm of Wagner and McGuigan, and the brothers Louis and Max Rosenthal.

The experiments of the Rosenthals and others were newly described as "chromolithography," and it is easy to imagine the growing excitement among both printers and readers with a sudden profusion of full color, rather than the customary black and white of most prints and books. The new color skills, which involved separate stones for each color and the difficult attendant

Peter Duval after Christian Schuessele, color lithograph on the added title page for John S. Hart, *The Iris: An Illuminated Souvenir.* Philadelphia, 1852. Graphic Arts.

problems of inking and registration, coincided with another printing phenomenon of the mid-nineteenth century, the "annual gift book" (see 1829, 1834). These poetic effusions, with such titles as *The Pearl*, *The Talisman*, *The Moss Rose*, and *The Iris*, peaked in popularity in the 1850s. Embellished by ultra fancy gold-stamped bindings and added chromolithograph title pages, the gift annuals quickly became essential status symbols for every culturally aware owner of an American parlor. *The Iris* of 1852 was richly indulgent, with twelve "gems of art" printed in full color chromo by Duval. Queen Victoria ordered a dozen copies, and called it "the prettiest work she had seen from America," adding that "it reflected great credit on the city of Philadelphia."*

* Nicholas B. Wainwright, *Philadelphia in the Romantic Age of Lithography* (Philadelphia, 1958).

Hammatt Billings, wood engraving on a handkerchief, showing Little Eva reading the Bible to Uncle Tom in the Arbor. Boston, 1852. Graphic Arts, The Sinclair Hamilton Collection.

· 1852 ·

The first edition of Harriet Beecher Stowe's *Uncle Tom's Cabin*, with "six elegant designs by Billings," appeared on March 20, 1852. The book became one of the fermenting agents in a growing movement to abolish slavery in the South. The pictures by Billings played a part in the drama of the years leading up to the Civil War, with his design of Uncle Tom and Little Eva reproduced and copied on everything from handkerchiefs to sheet-music covers. Thomas Strong's 1853 colored lithograph, "First Meeting of Uncle Tom and Eva," copies the figures but changes Billings' bower to a stereotypical Southern scene of cotton bales on the Mississippi.

Thomas W. Strong, colored lithograph, "First Meeting of Uncle Tom and Eva." New York, 1853. Graphic Arts.

Napoleon Sarony, lithograph for Stephen Foster, *Jeanie with the Light Brown Hair*. New York, 1854. Music Library.

· 1854 ·

The lithographic firm of Sarony and Major was one of several highly successful partnerships that characterized American lithography in the nineteenth century. Childs and Inman, Sarony and Major, and later, Currier and Ives, became flourishing printmaking enterprises. Lithography also now started to be far more versatile as an advertising medium. Publishers discovered that sheet music covers, embellished with chromos and lithotints, sold almost as fast as they could be printed. The lithographed cover of Stephen Foster's *Jeanie with the Light Brown Hair* rises well above routine advertising and is a perfect expression of popular art of its period, gently sentimental and sweetly simple, like the music itself.

William Sharp, chromolithograph, "American Water Lily," from John Fisk Allen, *Victoria Regia; or, The Great Water Lily of America.* Boston, 1854. Graphic Arts.

· 1854 ·

William Sharp emigrated from England to America in the late 1830s where he set up his own lithography shop in Boston. He had produced the first lithograph to be printed in colors in America by 1840,* several years before Peter Duval's color work in Philadelphia. But it was his later large-scale drawings on stone for John Fisk Allen's botanical folio, *Victoria Regia,* published in Boston in 1854, that gives William Sharp a distinct place in the development of successful chromolithography. Drawn with great decorative flair, four color plates illustrate the progressive stages towards the radiant flowering of the American water lily. Printed in the full size of the flower itself, Sharp's prints are, for one flower, the botanical representation of the careful observation and artistry that characterizes Audubon's *Birds of America.*

* A portrait of the Reverend R.W.P. Greenwood, printed in Boston, 1840.

"Hancock House, Boston," calotype frontispiece to *Homes of American Statesmen*. New York, 1854. Graphic Arts.

· 1854 ·

The first photograph to be used in an American book was this so-called "sun picture" of John Hancock's house in Boston. Although taken by an unknown photographer, its presence marks a graphic milestone in the history of book illustration. It is a very early use of an original tipped-in photograph made by the print process developed in England in 1839 by Henry Fox Talbot.

Rev. E. B. Hillard, "Samuel Downing," *The Last Men of the Revolution. A Photograph of Each from the Life, Together with Views of Their Homes Printed in Colors.* Hartford, Connecticut, 1864. Graphic Arts. Gift of Frank Jewett Mather, Jr.

· 1864 ·

Similar early realization of photography's power to preserve the past is found in another book that records not only old houses but old men still living who had actually fought in the American Revolution. Each veteran is interviewed in the text, and his home illustrated in color lithography. This drummer-boy of the Revolution and six other venerable survivors recount their memories of 1776, but it is the photographs that give this small book a strangely compelling life of its own.

John Sartain, colored engraving after George Caleb Bingham, *The County Election*. New York, 1854. Graphic Arts. Gift of Leonard L. Milberg, Class of 1953.

· 1854 ·

Engraved reproduction of masterpieces of American painting began very early. John Singleton Copley and Benjamin West were both published in grand folio format by John Boydell in London in the eighteenth century. The idea of print reproduction, the perfect democratic way to disseminate art, also caught on in the mid-nineteenth century when the American Art Union and the New York Gallery of Goupil et Cie. published a number of the best painters of the day. George Caleb Bingham's work was highly favored, and his quintessential American scenes appear in the best professional engraving of the day.

Fitzhugh Lane, colored lithograph, *View of Gloucester, Massachusetts*. Boston, 1855. Graphic Arts. Gift of Leonard L. Milberg, Class of 1953.

· 1855 ·

A flowering of lithography on a grand scale took place in the 1850s. Fitzhugh Lane was one of the important American artists who had emerged from apprenticeship in the earliest lithographic firms, and who now took on far more ambitious compositions. A new wave of American city views drawn on incredibly oversized stones began to appear, while aquatint engraving on copper began to lose favor. Mindful of their place in time, virtually every civic-minded township had its still peaceful steepled skyline lithographed, preserving at least in print an America soon to change.

Platt D. Babbitt (?), half-plate daguerreotype, "Niagara Falls." Niagara Falls, New York, ca. 1855. Lent by Jean Horblitt.

· ca. 1855 ·

Niagara Falls was always the great American tourist attraction, and as early as 1853, when Platt Babbitt set up a special pavilion at the best American viewpoint, the Falls proved to be highly photogenic. This rare half-plate daguerreotype is typical of Babbitt's work, which he sold to visitors who had been photographed unawares as they admired the great cascade. Pictures like these are the first of that most prolific of tourist trades, souvenirs of Niagara Falls.

Charles Risdon Day, color lithograph after Frederick Edwin Church's oil painting, *Niagara Falls*. London, 1857. Graphic Arts. Gift of Leonard L. Milberg, Class of 1953.

· 1857 ·

A much more technically refined color lithography had been developed in England by 1851. The Great Exhibition in London showed in the Crystal Palace such peerless color prints as those of David Roberts and Louis Haghe. Similar English lithographic prowess is demonstrated in a color print of one of Frederick Church's most spectacular paintings, his *Niagara Falls* of 1857. Both painting and print created a sensation, with the print beautifully demonstrating how well lithography could duplicate the color, meticulous brushwork, and atmospheric depth of the original painting.

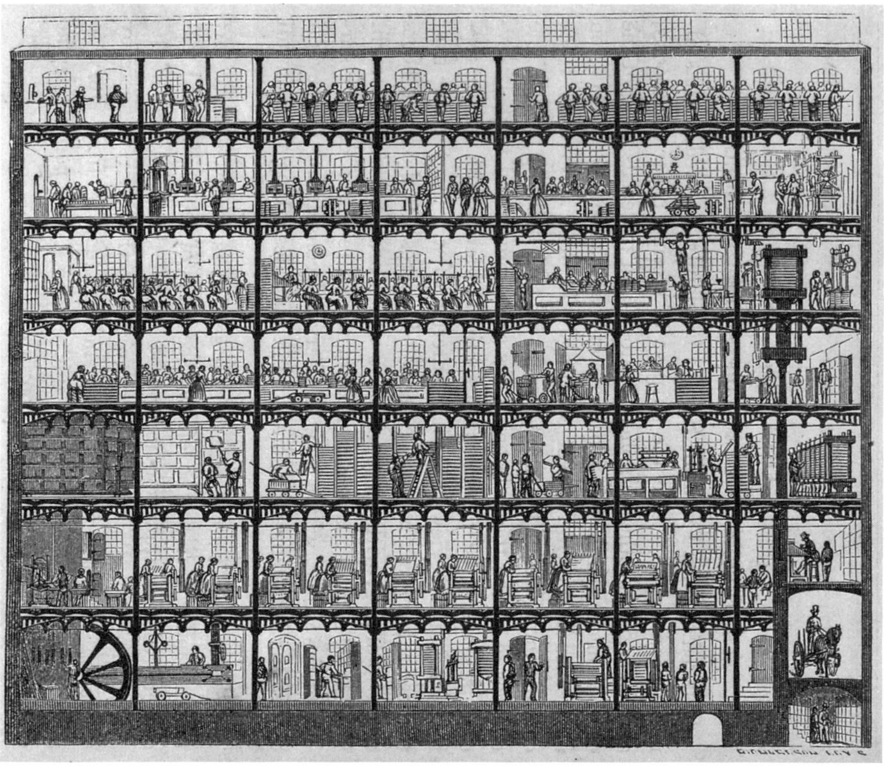

Jacob Abbott, "Interior of the Cliff Street Building," *The Harper Establishment; or, How the Story Books Are Made*. New York, 1855. Graphic Arts, The Elmer Adler Collection.

· 1855 ·

This small book written for children offers remarkable insight into the prodigious development of American printing by mid-century. The book offers a tour of Harper's seven-floor printing plant, looking in this cutaway drawing very much like the ant hill of activity that it very probably was. Type setting, printing, and all the attendant occupations of the making of books had now become an industry rather than a trade, and we are a long way from the Franklin hand press of a century earlier.

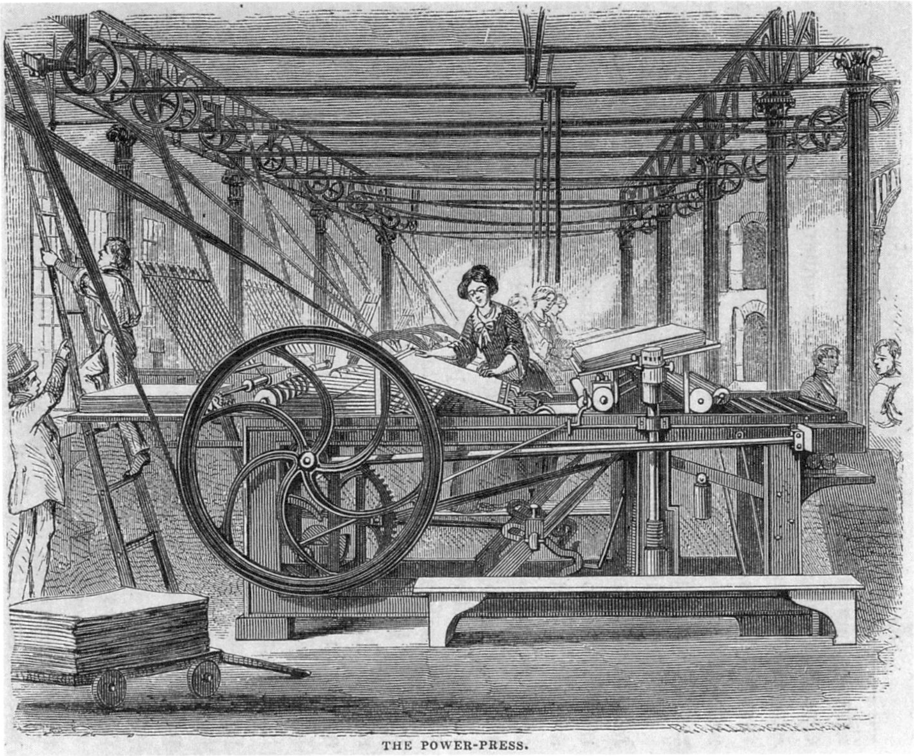

Jacob Abbott, "The Power Press," *The Harper Establishment; or, How the Story Books are Made.* New York, 1855. Graphic Arts, The Elmer Adler Collection.

· 1855 ·

Key to the expansion and success of printing as a new industry was the power press, with its vastly increased capacity for fast, economical production. With the added power of steam these presses seemed like machines for the "Sorcerer's Apprentice," churning out geometrically increased numbers of posters, books, and newspapers. The power press not only expanded printing production, but made the idea of pictorial journalism possible. Together with an insatiable public appetite for pictures, the first illustrated magazines appeared, including the *Illustrated London News* in England, and *Harper's Weekly* in America.

O. B. Brown, sheet music for "The Stars and Stripes." Boston, 1861. Graphic Arts.

· 1861 ·

The bombardment of Fort Sumter on April 12, 1861, rekindled already strong feelings of North against South. The Civil War began. But the idea of two flags was anathema to many, and the reaction inspired a surge of flag songs. "The Stars and Stripes," with its intricately color-printed cover in red and blue inks and still memorable lyrics of "Rally 'Round the Flag, Boys, Rally 'Round the Flag," helped galvanize the North to action.

George E. Perine, color engraving, *And the Star-Spangled Banner in Triumph Shall Wave. . . .* New York, 1862. Graphic Arts. *(detail)*

· 1862 ·

Rising patriotism, even in the parlor, is clear in this print of 1862. The same embellishment of crossed flags appears on the piano music, and a print of John Trumbull's *Battle of Bunker's Hill* hangs on the wall. Popular songs, such as Julia Ward Howe's great "Battle Hymn of the Republic," composed in 1861, did much to stir a divided nation in the growing crisis of war.

James Queen, chromolithograph, *The Volunteers in Defense of the Government against Usurpation.* Philadelphia, 1861. Graphic Arts.

· 1861 ·

The artist and lithographer of this emotionally charged scene was James Queen, one of the most gifted of Peter Duval's students in the new chromolithography. He rallied to the cause of the war with some of his best work, including this strong pyramidal design of flag and eager-to-march militiamen.

Stein and Jones, poster, "Volunteers Wanted . . . At Once!" Philadelphia, 1862. Rare Books.

· 1862 ·

The declaration of war coincided with dramatic developments in printing: the use of the steam-power press and ever bigger woodblock types. The combined result was a sudden expansion of the conventional broadside into a dramatic new graphic form, the wall-size poster. Patriotic fervor of the day helped to unleash a new "power of the press." Full of the biggest printed letter forms yet devised, these posters are typically surmounted by a proud woodcut emblem of the American eagle aggressively perched on a starred-and-striped shield.

Alexander Gardner, "The President and General McClellan, on the Battlefield of Antietam." New York, 1862. Graphic Arts.

· 1862 ·

Mathew Brady and Alexander Gardner were early photographers of true ability and vision who recognized the historic importance of documenting the Civil War with their cameras. They also recognized that the profile of President Lincoln was remarkably photogenic. Brady in particular left a priceless American legacy in his many portraits of the face of Lincoln. Documentation of military history through photography had strong beginnings in the work of these early American masters of the camera.

Timothy O'Sullivan or Alexander Gardner, photograph, "Special Artist, Harpers Ferry." Harpers Ferry, 1862. Graphic Arts.

The rapid reporting of the Civil War in pictures was unrivalled by any news event up to this time. Both photographers and artists were there to take photographs and draw pictures. In addition *Harper's Weekly* set up an assembly-line system of engraving wood blocks in sections after the designs sent from the front lines. The blocks were then bolted together and printed in the magazine at unheard-of speed. Alfred Waud, shown here sketching in the field, created thousands of drawings for *Harper's Weekly.* Much better known artists, Winslow Homer and Felix O.C. Darley, were also there to record the scene at first-hand.

(*Overleaf*) Wood engraving in several woodblocks with barely perceptible printing block seams, after Winslow Homer, "The War for the Union 1862, A Cavalry Charge," *Harper's Weekly*, July 5, 1862. Graphic Arts.

Panoramic colored lithograph, *Scenes of the Civil War*, rolled strip mounted in a toy theater box. New York, ca. 1864. Graphic Arts.

· 1864 ·

The popular press became much more active during and after the Civil War. Among the many graphic records of the conflict were such children's toys as this small cardboard theater containing a moving strip that shows the events of the war from the firing on Fort Sumter to the burning of Atlanta. Popular spy novels also appeared. *Pauline of the Potomac*, "an authentic and thrilling narrative of the beautiful and accomplished Miss Pauline d'Estrange," included "magnificently colored engravings executed specially for its pages." *Pauline of the Potomac* is an early example in both graphic format and melodramatic content of the later extremely popular "dime novels."

Pauline of the Potomac; or, General McClellan's Spy. Philadelphia, 1864. Graphic Arts, The Sinclair Hamilton Collection. ▶

Pauline
of the
POTOMAC
or
Gen.l McClellan's
Spy.
Philadelphia,
Verlag von Barclay u. Co.,
No. 56 Nord Sechste Straße.

Felix O.C. Darley, illustration on wood for James Gregory, *A Selection of War Lyrics*. New York, 1864. Graphic Arts, The Sinclair Hamilton Collection.

· 1864 ·

James Gregory's anthology of war poems followed swiftly on the end of the war and incorporated several drawings by the most celebrated illustrator of the day, Felix Darley. It is Darley's name that is gold-stamped on the cover, not the poet's, and Gregory does not even get credit on the title page. Darley was a fine draftsman and his best work compares well with that of the best European artists of the time. Too little known today, he was the accepted master of book illustration in the mid-nineteenth century.

Felix O.C. Darley, pencil drawing of a sentinel. Place and date unknown. Graphic Arts.

Winslow Homer, pencil drawing of Todd Lincoln, Abraham Lincoln, and General Grant. Signed "W. H." and dated 1865. Graphic Arts. Gift of Mrs. David A. Reed.

· 1865 ·

The lightly sketched background of flag and troops, and the drum in the foreground suggest that the setting here may well be a grand review of the victorious returning troops on May 23 and 24, 1865, in Washington. The frontispiece of *The Boys in Blue*, also shown here, is dated 1865 and is a far more labored picture of the same jubilant parade and celebration of surviving troops.

Augustus Robin after A. L. Rawson, engraving, "The Grand Review at Washington. . . . ," in Mrs. A. H. Hoge, *The Boys in Blue; or, Heroes of the 'Rank and File'.* New York, 1867. Graphic Arts, The Sinclair Hamilton Collection. ▶

THE BOYS IN BLUE. WELCOME HOME.
ENGRAVED EXPRESSLY FOR THE BOYS IN BLUE.
THE GRAND REVIEW AT WASHINGTON,
MAY 23D & 24TH 1865.

Currier and Ives, hand-colored lithograph after a painting by George Henry Durrie, *New England Winter Scene.* New York, 1864. Graphic Arts. Gift of Leonard L. Milberg, Class of 1953.

· 1864 ·

The postwar years ushered in a new age of peace and prosperity well exemplified in the color prints of the period. Currier and Ives of New York reigned supreme in the newly thriving market for lithographs, followed by Louis Prang of Boston, who shared Currier and Ives' profitable belief in "art for the people." Determined to develop the color printing begun in Philadelphia in the 1840s, Currier and Ives made their first valiant effort in true color lithography with *American Speckled Brook Trout.* Although it is a careful copy, the color printing made an aesthetic travesty of Arthur Tait's original painting, and the great effort involved discouraged Currier and Ives enough to persuade them to stay with the old tradition of hand-coloring thereafter.

Charles Parsons for Currier and Ives, chromolithograph after Arthur Tait's *American Speckled Brook Trout*. Graphic Arts, The Iconography Collection. Gift of Carl Otto von Kienbusch, Class of 1906.

· 1864 ·

The inadequate color reproduction of Tait's *American Speckled Brook Trout* also displeased the artist, and he was easily persuaded by Currier and Ives' Boston rival, Louis Prang and Co., to create a design for them. Tait produced another nature theme, a group of chicks, which became Prang's first published color print. Although its appearance in 1866 provoked high critical distaste, the print was an enormous popular success. What the critics dismissed as "cheap chromos" proved to be a vast new popular market. Art and sentiment in inexpensive full color proved irresistible. Sold at first in the thousands, then by the millions, Prang prints began the American "chromo age."

Louis Prang, chromolithograph trade card. Boston, no date. Graphic Arts.

· 1874 ·

The development of color printing by lithography, like so many of the graphic arts in America, was primarily the achievement of immigrant artists and printmakers from Europe. William Sharp, who came from London to Boston in 1830, produced that same year the first American color lithography, and later his best work, the "Great Water Lily of America." (see 1854) Philadelphia, New York, and Cincinnati soon followed as centers for immigrant lithographers determined to capture in print the elusive but very real charms of color. The most important group of these pioneer color printmakers in Philadelphia included the German immigrants, Louis and Max Rosenthal, and the French-born Peter Duval. (see 1851, 1852) But it was the German, Louis Prang, who had fled Europe in the revolution of 1848, who truly recognized both the artistic and big-business potential of this powerful infant of color printing, the "chromo." Inventing the greeting card in the 1870s, Prang went on to turn the reproduction of art in color into a new printing industry. In the process he became a wealthy patron and collector, and through his books, Prang art supplies, and chromo prints, a powerful force in the dissemination of American art.

Louis Prang, chromolithograph, "Lithographer," from *Prang's Aids for Object Teaching*. Boston, 1874. Graphic Arts. (*detail*)

Winslow Homer, wood engraving, "Snap-the-Whip," from *Harper's Weekly*, September 20, 1873. Graphic Arts, The Sinclair Hamilton Collection. (*detail*)

· 1873 ·

For years after the Civil War, illustrations for *Harper's Weekly* still included double-page spreads by Winslow Homer, but instead of battle scenes the American schoolyard is portrayed in images still full of energy but now flooded with sunlight. Such light-suffused subjects of American boyhood became a favorite Homer theme, with his wash drawing often translated into the pure line of wood engraving by true virtuosos of the medium.

Winslow Homer, "You Want to See My Pa, I S'pose," silhouette design for the binding of James Russell Lowell, *The Courtin'*. Boston, 1874. Graphic Arts, The Sinclair Hamilton Collection.

· 1874 ·

Winslow Homer, with all of his great gifts, was also a fine book artist. He illustrated not only such popular journals as *Ballou's Pictorial*, *Riverside Magazine*, and *Harper's Weekly*, but also a number of books.* Beginning in 1857 with *Ballou's Pictorial*, Homer contributed countless illustrations, often with an element of experimentation. He gave unexpected wit to designs for his first book of 1858, *Three Blind Mice*, and ventured into pure silhouette for the binding design and pictures for Lowell's *The Courtin'* of 1874.

* Frank Jewett Mather, "Winslow Homer as Book Illustrator, with a Descriptive Checklist," *Princeton University Library Chronicle*, Vol. 1, No. 1 (November 1939) 15–32.

Thomas Moran, wood engraving after his drawing of Chicago Lake, Colorado, in William Cullen Bryant, ed., *Picturesque America, or the Land We Live In.* New York, 1875. Graphic Arts, The Sinclair Hamilton Collection.

· 1875 ·

The scenic wonders of America in general and the grandeur of the West in particular were celebrated in an ambitious publishing venture of 1875, *Picturesque America, or the Land We Live In.* Issued in forty-eight parts, this is one of the best of American illustrated books for its beautifully executed wood engravings after the designs of Harry Fenn, Thomas Moran, and others. The fulsome text was edited by William Cullen Bryant, but it is the pictures that truly show the best of American scenery before the soon-to-arrive smokestacks of the Industrial Age. While it is the last of several similar projects dating as far back as the eighteenth century—*Scenographia Americana* (see 1768), Joshua Shaw's *Picturesque Views of American Scenery* (1820), and William Bartlett's *American Scenery* (1840)—this work at last escapes the traditional British viewpoint, and is perhaps the most honest American scenery of them all.

Louis Prang, chromolithograph after Thomas Moran's watercolor, "Mosquito Trail, Rocky Mountains of Colorado," from Ferdinand Hayden, The *Yellowstone National Park*. Boston, 1875. The Princeton Collections of Western Americana. Gift of J. Monroe Thorington, Class of 1915.

· 1875 ·

The wood engravings of *Picturesque America* were successful, but limited to black and white. For Ferdinand Hayden, the government geologist who explored the Yellowstone Valley in 1871, such pictures were like seeing "Hamlet with the role of Hamlet omitted," and he decided to give the watercolors made by his expedition artist, Thomas Moran, to the best of all American color lithographers, Louis Prang of Boston, for full-color reproduction. The results exceeded his fondest hopes. As he rightly wrote in his preface, "It is a just subject for national pride to see a work of this character, which takes equal rank with anything of the kind ever undertaken in Europe, produced wholly on American soil."

William Henry Jackson, wet-plate photograph, "Twin Lake, Big Cottonwood Canon [*sic*], Utah." Place unknown, 1874. Graphic Arts.

· 1874 ·

Photography of the American West followed soon after the discovery of gold in 1849. The daguerreotypes of that time were replaced, in the 1870s, by the dramatic scenic work in oversize wet-plate prints by Timothy O'Sullivan and William Henry Jackson. Jackson accompanied Dr. Ferdinand Hayden on his historic official exploration of Utah, Colorado, and Wyoming, and despite the fragile glass-plate negatives and cumbersome equipment of early photography, Jackson produced folio-size prints of extraordinary quality. His prints helped greatly in the campaign to persuade Congress to create Yellowstone National Park in 1872.

Edward Long (?), chromolithograph after Albert Bierstadt, *The Rocky Mountains, Landers Peak*. Place unknown, no date. Lent by Alfred L. Bush. (*detail*)

Not only photographers but also serious painters began to recognize that the scenery of the West was a highly suitable subject for art. Artists such as Albert Bierstadt depicted the grandeur of the mountainous West in splendid scenes like his "Rocky Mountains, Landers Peak," exhibited in New York's Metropolitan Museum of Art in 1863 amid Bierstadt's collection of Indian artifacts and an actual wigwam. The huge painting was a popular sensation, rivalling the equally spectacular painting hanging at the same gallery, Frederick Church's *Heart of the Andes*. Like several other Bierstadt paintings, it was later reproduced in elaborate chromolithography, using as many as twenty colors.

Clay, Cossack, and Co., chromolithograph after a painting by Archibald Willard, *Yankee Doodle*. Buffalo, 1876. Graphic Arts.

· 1876 ·

National pride, which had been building for a full century, crested in the great International Centennial Exposition held in Philadelphia from May to November of 1876. The buildings covered twenty acres in Fairmount Park and were visited by nearly ten million people. The new chromo industry produced an extravaganza of printed souvenirs ranging from small "trade cards" advertising every conceivable product to such popular blockbuster chromos as *Yankee Doodle*, now known as *The Spirit of '76*. This super-patriotic image of two drummers and a fifer bravely marching in step in the midst of battle became an instant sensation and the most hopelessly popular of all American chromos even until recent times.

"Philadelphia International-Exhibition," a "Stevengraph" woven image in silk. Coventry, England, 1876. Graphic Arts.

· 1876 ·

Among the multitude of souvenirs of the Centennial were several small "Stevens pure silk woven pictures." Made in Coventry, England, such curios enjoyed a short-lived vogue in the Victorian age, mainly as fancy bookmarks. They are also interesting as attractive relics of a miniature version of the Jacquard loom, which wove textile designs programmed from punch cards—an idea that would eventually lead to the modern computer.

Anonymous, wood engraving, "Photo-electrotyping," *Scientific American*, October 2, 1880. New York, 1880. Graphic Arts.

· 1880 ·

By the 1880s printing had become an increasingly diversified major American industry. Every town of any size had its own printer, both for letterpress and lithography. New inventions soon included such significant improvements as the halftone screen developed by Frederick Ives in Philadelphia* and the linotype typesetting machine invented in 1885 by Ottmar Mergenthaler in New York. The hand-engraved woodblock also began to be replaced by the photographic linecut, marking the beginning of the end for one of the nineteenth century's largest artistic trades.

* Ives also developed in the 1880s the three-color separation halftone process that is still in use today.

Woodcut poster for "Thomas Brown, Dealer in Hats, Caps, Boots, and Shoes. . . ." Princeton, New Jersey, ca. 1880. Graphic Arts.

· ca. 1880 ·

Advertising in print emerged as a national obsession in the 1880s, resulting in the proliferation of "job-printers" and leading to the nationwide spread of printing in America. Small-town printers from Akron to Poughkeepsie gave their communities not only information of every kind, but often added a certain sense of style to their work. These men had their own journal, the *American Model Printer*, which supplied both technical and aesthetic advice. The bizarre letterforms, eccentric angular typography, and neo-Egyptian ornaments so characteristic of American graphic design of the 1880s may be blamed in part on the examples and advice found in the *American Model Printer.*

Chromolithographed trade cards for "Wisner's Tiger, the King of Rakes," and "Sapolio Soap." New York, ca. 1882. Graphic Arts.

· ca. 1882 ·

Perhaps the most pervasive part of the "chromo age" of the 1880s was the trade card. These deceptively innocent little cards, printed in color lithography, represent a Victorian flowering of one of the most fertile ideas of the printing trades, advertising. Two developments in printing, the jobbing press and the cheap chromolithograph, helped to sow this dragon-seed. Unlimited printing of the advertising trade card—along with its folio-sized big brother, the poster—represented new celebrations of the marketplace and was still another massive step in the democratization of imagery. With true hucksterism, the cards linked soap with Uncle Sam, cure-all medicines with Columbia, or flying tigers with farm machinery. Like Currier and Ives prints and Prang chromos, here was another far-reaching presentation of "pictures for the people."

Anonymous, colored engraving, "Godey's Fashions," in *Godey's Lady's Book*. New York, 1883. Graphic Arts.

· 1883 ·

The trade cards of the 1880s not only began endless pictorial huckstering of soap, toothpaste, and nerve tonics, but also exploited all the minority stereotypes. Irish, Jews, Chinese, and Blacks all found themselves treated with little kindness. Women were also stereotyped, but a new image began to appear. *Godey's Lady's Book* for 1883 includes a machine, the "calligraphic typewriter," for the new office working class, the secretary. Historic events are also depicted, with many trade cards linking advertising with the opening of the Brooklyn Bridge in 1883 and the arrival of the Statue of Liberty in 1886. By 1889 trade cards showed the telephone, the electric light, and the first Otis elevator working to transform American life forevermore.

A. Major, color lithograph, "Bird's-Eye View of the Great New York and Brooklyn Bridge, and Grand Display of Fireworks on Opening Night." New York, 1883. Lent by Leonard L. Milberg, Class of 1953.

Forbes Co., color lithograph trade card for Willimantic Thread. Boston, no date. Graphic Arts.

· 1883 ·

The engineering marvel of a great bridge across the East River from Manhattan to Brooklyn gave New York City and the nation a new symbol suggesting the limitless progress of the future. Designed by John Augustus Roebling, the Brooklyn Bridge opened in 1883 with a display of fireworks and celebration. It became an instant American icon, appearing not only in prints, but also as a favorite trade card gimmick for everything from Willimantic sewing thread to Lydia Pinkham pills.

Elihu Vedder, drawing and binding design for *The Rubáiyát of Omar Khayyám*. Boston, 1884. Graphic Arts. Gift of Sinclair Hamilton, Class of 1906.

· 1884 ·

The excesses of chromo advertising and the increasing ugliness of the industrial age led to a rebirth of aestheticism both in Europe and America in the 1880s. Oscar Wilde made his notorious American lecture tour in 1882, scolding Americans for their hopelessly bad taste, while France and the rest of Europe bloomed with a new international style, *art nouveau*. One artist in America, Elihu Vedder, embodied the new style in a remarkably lavish limited edition of the *Rubáiyát*, with two hundred illustrations printed on Japanese paper, flowered silk doublures, and a gold-stamped binding design of startling originality for its date. The work is conceived on a grand scale and printed in a folio format rarely seen in books of poetry. Vedder was a visionary artist, ahead of his time, and one of the first expatriate artists to settle in Rome.

Francesca Alexander, pen and ink drawing of a young girl. Rome, no date. Graphic Arts. Gift of Arthur C. Holden, Class of 1912.

· 1885 ·

The American artist abroad was a cultural tradition from Benjamin West and his followers in the eighteenth century to the American school, evoked by Nathaniel Hawthorne in *The Marble Faun*, set in Rome in the 1860s. Less well known is a small Anglo-American colony in Italy headed by Francesca Alexander, whose artist father, Francis King Alexander, abandoned Boston for Rome in 1853. Francesca became an artist in her own right, was a close friend of John Ruskin, and published a fine illustrated book, *Roadside Songs of Tuscany*, in 1885.

James Abbott McNeill Whistler, etching, "The Bridge," from a set of twenty-six etchings of Venice. London, 1886. Graphic Arts. Gift of David H. McAlpin III, Class of 1920.

· 1886 ·

In the last decades of the nineteenth century, several of the most gifted of American artists fled the excesses of the chromo and industrial civilization of America for the well-established culture of Europe. Both John Singer Sargent and James A. McNeill Whistler settled in England as lifelong expatriates. The democratic idea of "pictures for the people" was changed by Whistler, who pursued deliberate elitism in prints by producing limited editions for the gratification of the few. A new militant aestheticism was presented by Whistler to a bourgeois society. He infuriated John Ruskin—and won a famous lawsuit against the venerable Victorian critic. With deliberate preciosity, he signed his limited-edition prints on a special tab with his signature-monogram, a butterfly.

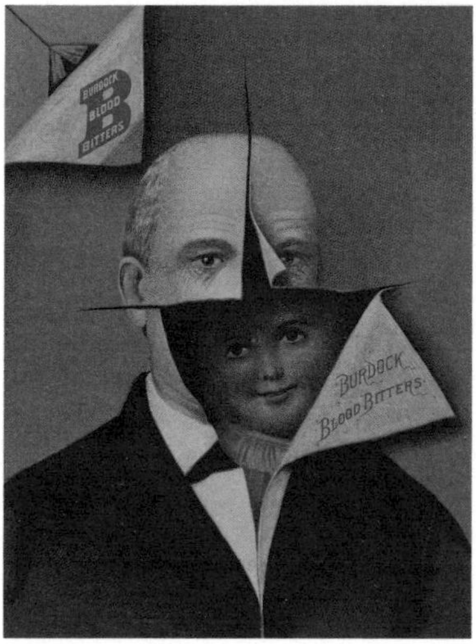

Clay and Cosack, chromolithography trade card "At 6 and at 60." Buffalo, New York, ca. 1887. Lent by Paul M. Ingersoll, Class of 1950.

· 1887 ·

Amid all the aesthetic turmoil of advertising trade cards, circus posters, and tourist souvenirs a few chromo images of artistic and expressive force can be discovered. A painting of unusual realism, *The Old Violin* by the New York painter William Harnett, was exhibited at the Cincinnati Industrial Fair in 1886. A well-established Cincinnati lithographer, Frank Tuchfarber, purchased the painting with the intention of reproducing it by his own chromolithography. The resulting print, published in both Cincinnati and Covington, Kentucky, was an immediate sales success. It was and still remains popular art at its best, easily understood at first glance, yet as fully charged with other meanings as is the original Harnett painting.

Another strangely evocative chromolithograph, this time a trade card by a rival firm of lithographers, Clay and Cosack, advertises a health tonic, Burdock's Blood Bitters. It is also very much in the tradition of William Harnett's *trompe l'oeil* realism. This carefully rendered design portrays a youthful soul revealed in the slashed canvas of a portrait of an old man. More than an advertising stunt, it is a haunting mystical image, worthy of the modern Belgian master of surrealism, René Magritte.

Frank Tuchfarber after William Harnett, chromolithograph, *The Old Violin.* Cincinnati, 1887; reprinted by Donaldson Art Sign Co., Covington, Kentucky, 1887. Graphic Arts.

Eadward Muybridge, *Animal Locomotion: Electro Photographic Investigations of Consecutive Phases of Animal Movement.* Philadelphia, 1887. Rare Books.

· 1887 ·

Before Muybridge, artists depicted a running horse with all legs outstretched in a "flying gallop." Using a series of "stop-motion" photographs achieved by a camera-lined track, Muybridge proved for the first time that artists, for all their powers of observation, had it wrong, and that a horse's gallop had a totally different pattern. Recognizing a whole new area of visual exploration, Muybridge worked for three years at the University of Pennsylvania to produce his monumental study, *Animal Locomotion.* In some 100,000 stop-motion photographs, Muybridge presented to American art and science not only a great illustrated book on kinaesthetics, but the practical key to the dream of dreams, moving pictures.

Thomas Eakins, photograph, "The Swimming Hole." Philadelphia, ca. 1888. Lent by the Art Museum, Princeton University.

· ca. 1888 ·

Thomas Eakins, as head of the Pennsylvania Academy of the Fine Arts, invited Eadward Muybridge to lecture on his motion photography in 1883. Eakins was himself an excellent photographer, and did his own Muybridge-like multiple-exposure experiments in photography. As an artist Eakins was particularly disposed to painting and photographing the nude. His sensitive photography of the body, like Muybridge's thousands of similar studies, are surprising in the Philadelphia of the 1880s. Eventually, Eakins' persistent use of such models in his painting classes led to his historically outrageous dismissal by officials of the Academy.

Howard Pyle, "While I lay there with my horse upon me. . . . ," in his *Otto of the Silver Hand*. New York, 1888. Graphic Arts. Gift of Frank Jewett Mather, Jr.

· 1888 ·

The development of electroplate printing was a turning point in book illustration, freeing the artist from the intermediary hand of the wood engraver. Book illustration in pen and ink line work soon developed as a style of its own. Howard Pyle was one of the first American artists to exploit the pure line potential of drawings now appearing regularly in literary journals such as *Harper's Monthly* and *Scribner's Magazine*. Pyle had been discovered by the important Harper art editor, Charles Parsons, and soon emerged as the leading illustrator of the period. A great teacher as well as artist, he went on to establish his own schools of illustration in both Philadelphia and in Wilmington, Delaware, creating a group of American "picture makers" that would include Violet Oakley, Jessie Willcox Smith, Maxfield Parrish, and N. C. Wyeth. Pyle was the beginning of a "golden age" of American literary illustration that would eventually spawn the Brandywine tradition of serious painting as illustration.

Mary Cassatt, color aquatint, "*The Coiffure*," signed in pencil. Paris, 1891. Graphic Arts, The Elmer Adler Collection.

· 1891 ·

Mary Cassatt left Philadelphia to study art in Paris in 1865 with her father's farewell remark: "I'd rather see you dead." Instead, she found independence and direction for her life. Like Whistler in many ways, she found inspiration in Japanese art, and pursued printmaking as a major expression. Dry point and aquatint became particular skills, and in 1890–1891, Mary Cassatt published a series of ten color aquatint prints showing the everyday life of a nineteenth-century woman. The series demonstrates both her complete absorption in Japanese style and her consummate mastery of the color print. Adelyn Breeskin wrote of them: "They are indeed her most original contribution, adding a new chapter to the history of the graphic arts, and as color prints, have never been surpassed."

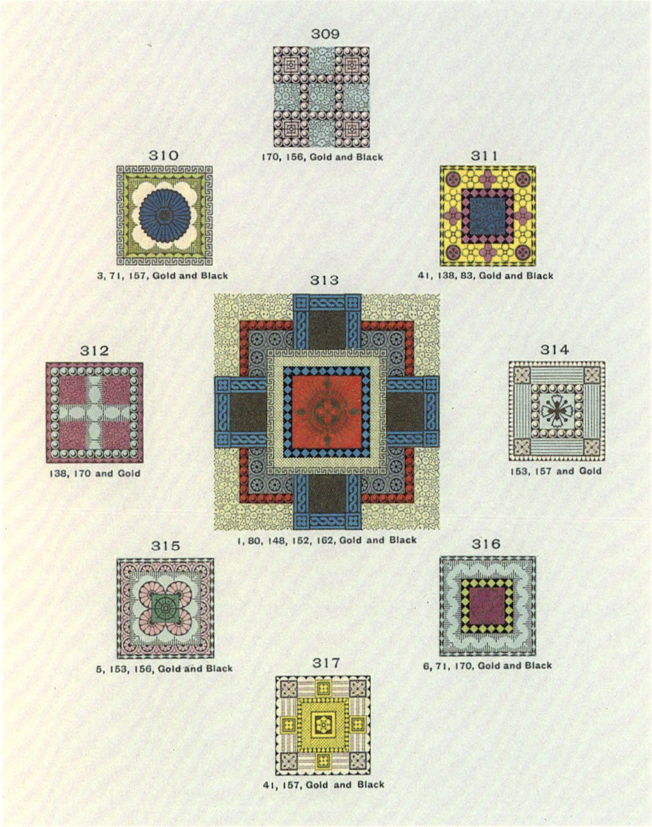

John F. Earhart, a combination of colors and tints with gold, from *The Color Printer, A Treatise on the Use of Colors in Typographic Printing*. Cincinnati, Ohio, 1892. Graphic Arts, The Elmer Adler Collection.

· 1892 ·

The use of color in typography and graphic design found its first use in printing in America in the work of John Mycall in the late eighteenth century (see 1789). A full century later, John Earhart, following the lead of Cincinnati color-printer John Strowbridge, took typographic color to new limits. Earhart pursued the subtleties of half-tone tints and the interaction of colors to produce a book full of precise, jewel-like patterns that recall the work of Owen Jones and his *Grammar of Ornament* in England. Although Earhart was more craftsman than artist, he gave printing one of its most definitive texts on the use of color.

Tourist brochure for the World's Columbian Exposition. Chicago, 1893. Graphic Arts.

· 1893 ·

The four-hundredth anniversary of the discovery of America was the occasion of renewed historical awareness and nationalistic pride in the promise of America, and was the inspiration for the World's Columbian Exposition of 1893. Renewed appreciation of classical architectural styles resulted in an eclectic mix of 150 buildings in Greek and Roman, Romanesque, and Renaissance architecture, all constructed in a pseudo-marble material known as "staff." This short-lived architectural fantasy, called the "White City," was the work of many of the best *beaux arts* architects of the period, including Charles F. McKim, William R. Mead, and Stanford White, as well as Louis Sullivan and other shapers of the American city skyline of the next century.

Robert Anning Bell and Bertram Goodhue, "Easter Day," illustration and border design for Daniel Berkeley Updike's printing of *The Altar Book* (Book of Common Prayer). Boston, 1896. Graphic Arts. (*detail*)

· 1896 ·

Daniel Berkeley Updike was at first an American follower of William Morris, adopting for his printing design the same manner of design motifs and the superior craftsmanship of Morris' Kelmscott Press in England. His *Altar Book* includes borders, initials, and binding designed by Bertram Goodhue, and illustrations by Robert Anning Bell. Both end-of-the-century *art nouveau* and Pre-Raphaelite influences are here given American expression, making this handsome folio a good example of the international style prevailing among artists of the time. Updike would go on to become the leading book designer of America in the early twentieth century, and a major typographer, private press printer, and later the author of a major history of printing, *Printing Types, Their History, Forms and Use* (Cambridge, 1922).

Will H. Bradley, poster broadside for *Bradley His Book*. Springfield, Massachusetts, 1896. Graphic Arts.

· 1896 ·

The serpentine contours of *art nouveau* are everywhere in the graphic art of one of America's best *fin de siècle* artists, Will Bradley. His book illustrations and advertising designs merge in one style, and automobile tires, toothpaste, and bicycles are presented with the same curvilinear, highly energized style as his more serious book illustration. Bradley revolutionized poster and advertising design, rejecting homely Victorian styles for the latest cosmopolitan influences of Alphonse Mucha and Aubrey Beardsley.

William Thomas Smedley, water-color, "De moon come' out. . . . ," reproduced in the Charles Scribner illustrated edition of Thomas Nelson Page, *In Ole Virginia*. New York, 1896. Graphic Arts. Gift of Charles Scribner III, Class of 1973.

· 1896 ·

The half-tone screen, developed by Frederick Ives and others, expanded the expressive potential of magazine illustration as an art form. *Harper's Monthly* and *Scribner's Magazine* became not only patrons of American writers, but of illustrators as well. Far less snobbish distinctions between fine art and illustration made cultural celebrities of Howard Pyle and Maxfield Parrish, and also less well remembered, but highly skilled artists like Robert Frederick Blum and William Smedley. Both Blum and Smedley were outstanding as water color painters, and moved between art and illustration just as easily as Winslow Homer had a generation earlier.

Charles Dana Gibson, charcoal drawing of a young woman. Signed and dated, New York, 1899. Graphic Arts.

· 1899–1900 ·

By the end of the century the ever-growing medium of the popular press began to reach truly expansive proportions. One of the ultimate American popular arts, the comic strip, began in 1897 with Rudolph Dirks' "Katzenjammer Kids." Thomas Nast broke the corruption of New York's Tammany Hall and Boss Tweed through his relentless political cartoons, and a new form of sophisticated cartooning art appeared in the drawings of Charles Dana Gibson. His "Gibson Girl" was the new woman. Her classic profile, flowing hair, and free spirit caught the national imagination. As the "Gibson Girl," she became an American national heroine, and her creator a wealthy man. She was a beautiful transitional creation, summing up the ever expanding popular imagery of the nineteenth century while being a graceful harbinger of the century to come.

Afterword

THIS three-century chronology of books, prints, and drawings does not represent a random selection of images, but rather a curator's attempt to put into recognizable order several important developments in American history and culture as depicted in the graphic arts. The selections are intended to be seen as far more than wearisome dates and routine texts; they are a sequential gathering of those books, prints, and drawings at Princeton that give the most authentic graphic and visual embodiment to North America's past. Included are images of America's discovery, its original inhabitants, flora, fauna, and landscape, its several wars, and its gradual achievement of political and cultural independence from Europe. These themes and others recur in successive waves in the history of American graphic arts, all complex and important enough to have been described again and again in the history books, but often misunderstood in their authentic pictorial representation. Study of these important books and prints yields a recognition of certain visual works as the true classics of their time and subject. Such classic works have long been recognized in literature, but less so in printed pictures. Librarians and scholars, however, have begun to recognize that the picture-book and print may convey complex information as surely as the often difficult semantics of the text.

Pictures have a "syntax" of their own, and present a complex mixture of iconography, technique, style, and most interesting of all, the artist's subjective interpretation of what he sees and portrays. To better understand book illustration, therefore, it is helpful to place it in its exact context, and it is one of the great virtues of books that such information is almost always firmly established on title page and colophon. Date established, techniques follow easily, presenting their own fascinating development. The discovery and mastery of the printing problems of line, tone, texture, light and shade, and finally color are all stories unto themselves, first in Asia, then in Europe, then in a last reprise, America.

In both the Old and the New World, woodcut, intaglio engraving (including mezzotint and aquatint), lithography, and photography, all have their own development. The multiple strands of the history of each of these printing techniques may be found in this catalogue, along with the emergence of new independence in both politics and art. The most difficult technique, but artistically one of the most important of them all—printing in color—is emphasized here. Included are many rare and little known examples, from the pioneer achievements of Gustave Peters in color woodcut to the beginnings of color lithography in the work of the Rosenthals, Peter Duval, and Thomas Sinclair in Philadelphia to the experiments of William Sharp and the full lush chromos of Louis Prang in Boston. Then, following a descent into the aesthetic maelstrom of advertising trade cards and circus posters, the century ends in the fine color typography of John Earhart and the consummate color aquatint prints of Mary Cassatt.

The many year-by-year entries of the catalogue also record in their chronological context our earliest scientific illustration from Mark Catesby and William Bartram to John James Audubon and Alfred M. Hoffy. The Revolution and the Civil War are here as well, very well documented by Princeton's extraordinary holdings for both periods. The growing country is illustrated from stage coach and steamboat travel to the discovery of the scenic wonders of the American West. Selected prints from the Leonard L. Milberg Collection of American City Views suggest a vast study in itself—the urbanization of America. Finally, among several other pictorial asides too good not to include, are the several entries related to the history of Princeton itself, from the first Dawkins view of 1764 to the Nassau Street haberdashery woodcut poster of 1883.

As Professor Arthur Link has said, "All history begins at home. . . . Without a sense of history, we have no sense of time, without a sense of time, we have no sense of place, and without time and place we have no sense of identity." The graphic arts in and of America help confirm that irreplaceable legacy—our cultural identity.

Bibliography

American Antiquarian Society, *A Society's Chief Joys, An Exhibition from the Collections of the American Antiquarian Society.* Worcester, Massachusetts, 1969.

American Printmaking before 1876. Washington, D.C., 1975.

Arader, W. Graham, III. *Native Grace: Prints of the New World 1590–1876.* Charlottesville, Virginia, 1988.

Axelrod, Alan, editor. *American Frontier Life: Early Western Painting and Prints.* Fort Worth, Texas, 1987.

Baker, W. S. *American Engravers and Their Works.* Philadelphia, 1875.

Beall, Karen F., comp. *American Prints in the Library of Congress.* Baltimore, 1970.

Bell, Whitfield J., Jr. *Early American Science.* Williamsburg, Virginia, 1955.

Bennett, Whitman. *A Practical Guide to American Nineteenth-Century Color Plate Books.* New York, 1949.

Best, James J. *American Popular Illustration.* Westport, Connecticut, 1984.

Brigham, Clarence S. *Fifty Years of Collecting Americana for the Library of The American Antiquarian Society 1908–1958.* Worcester, Massachusetts, 1958.

Bumgardner, Georgia, editor. *American Broadsides.* Barre, Massachusetts, 1971.

Comstock, Helen. "The Rediscovery of George Harvey," *Connoisseur,* Vol. 122 (1949) 120–121.

——. "Watercolors in the Hudson River Portfolio," *Connoisseur,* Vol. 120 (1947) 42–43.

Cowdrey, Mary Bartlett. "William Henry Bartlett and the American Scene," *New York History,* (1941) 388–400.

Cresswell, Donald H., comp. *The American Revolution in Drawings and Prints.* Washington, D.C., 1975.

Davidson, Marshall B. *Life in America,* 2 volumes. Boston, 1951.

Deák, Gloria-Gilda. *American Views, Prospects and Vistas.* New York, 1976.

——. *Picturing America, 1497–1899. Prints, Maps, and Drawings Bearing*

on the New World Discoveries and on the Development of the Territory that is now the United States. Princeton, New Jersey, 1988.
——. *William James Bennett, Master of the Aquatint View*. New York, 1988.
Dolmetsch, Joan D. *Eighteenth-Century Prints in Colonial America*. Williamsburg, Virginia, 1979.
Dow, Charles Mason. *Anthology and Bibliography of Niagara Falls*. Albany, New York, 1921.
Drepperd, Carl W. *Early American Prints*. New York and London, 1930.
Fern, Alan, and Milton Kaplan. *Viewpoints: A Selection from the Pictorial Collections of the Library of Congress*. Washington, D.C., 1975.
Fielding, Mantle. *American Engravers upon Copper and Steel*. Philadelphia, 1917.
Flexner, James Thomas. *History of American Painting*, 3 volumes. New York, 1962.
Fowble, E. McSherry. *Two Centuries of Prints in America 1680–1880*. Charlottesville, Virginia, 1987.
Gassan, Arnold. *A Chronology of Photography*. Athens, Ohio, 1972.
Groce, George C., and David H. Wallace. *The New-York Historical Society's Dictionary of Artists in America, 1564–1860*. New Haven and London, 1957.
Hahler, Christine Anne, editor. "*. . . Illustrated by Darley." An Exhibition of Original Drawimgs*. Wilmington, Delaware, 1978.
Hall, Elton W., editor. *American Maritime Prints*. New Bedford, Massachusetts, 1985.
Halsey, R. T. *"Impolitical Prints," The American Revolution as Pictured by Contemporary English Caricaturists*. New York, 1939.
Hamilton, Sinclair. *Early American Book Illustrators and Wood Engravers, 1670–1870*, 2 volumes. Princeton, New Jersey, 1968.
Historical Society of Princeton. *A Pleasant Likeness: Portraits and Landscapes of Central New Jersey, 1770–1920*. Catalogue of an exhibition. Princeton, New Jersey, 1989.
Hornung, Clarence P., and Fridolf Johnson. *200 Years of American Graphic Art*. New York, 1976.
Koke, Richard J., comp. *American Landscape and Genre Paintings in the New-York Historical Society*, 3 volumes. New York and Boston, 1982.
Lane, Wheaton J. *Pictorial History of Princeton*. Princeton, New Jersey, 1947.
Lewis, Benjamin M. *A Guide to Engravings in American Magazines, 1741–1810*. New York, 1959.
Lorant, Stefan, editor. *The New World; The First Pictures of America, Made by John White and Jacques Le Moyne and Engraved by Theodore Bry. . . .* New York, 1946.

Mann, Maybelle. "American Landscape Prints," *Art and Antiques*, Vol. 4 (1981) 90–99.
Marble, Annie Russell. *From 'Prentice to Patron, The Life Story of Isaiah Thomas*. New York, 1935.
Meyer, Susan E. *America's Great Illustrators*. New York, 1978.
Morse, John D., editor. *Prints In and Of America to 1850*. Charlottesville, Virginia, 1970.
Murrell, William. *A History of American Graphic Humor*. 2 volumes. New York, 1933.
Nash, Chauncey C. "John Warner Barber and His Books," *Walpole Society Note Book* (1934) 30–60.
Nichols, Charles L. *Isaiah Thomas*. Boston, 1912.
Nipps, Karen. *Naturally Fond of Pictures*. Philadelphia, 1989.
O'Gorman, James F., editor. *Apects of American Printmaking, 1800–1950*. New York, 1988.
Peck, Glenn C. *America in Print*, 1796–1941. New York, 1981.
Peters, Harry T. *America on Stone*. New York, 1931.
Reed, Walt, and Roger Reed. *The Illustrator in America, 1880–1980*. New York, 1984.
Reps, John W. *Cities on Stone: Nineteenth-Century Lithograph Images of the Urban West*. Fort Worth, Texas, 1976.
Rossiter, Henry P., ed. *M. and M. Karolik Collection of American Water Colors and Drawings, 1800–1875*. Boston, 1962.
Roylance, Dale R. "American Graphic Arts," *Princeton University Library Chronicle*, Vol. 42, No. 2 (Winter 1981).
——. "The Early Prints of New Haven," *New Haven: A Portfolio for the Bicentennial*. New Haven, Connecticut, 1976.
Rutherfurd, Livingston. *John Peter Zenger, His Press, His Trial, and a Bibliography of Zenger Imprints*. New York, 1904.
Shadwell, Wendy J. *American Printmaking, The First 150 Years*. Washington, D.C., 1969.
Shelley, Donald A. "George Harvey and His Atmospheric Landscapes of North America," *New-York Historical Society Quarterly*, Vol. 31 (April 1948) 104–113.
——. "William Guy Wall and His Watercolors for the Historic Hudson River Portfolio," *New-York Historical Society Quarterly*, Vol. 31 (January 1947) 25–45.
Sherman, Constance D. "A French Explorer [Jacques-Gerard Milbert] in the Hudson River Valley," *New-York Historical Society Quarterly*, Vol. 45 (July 1961) 255–280.
Silver, Rollo G. *The American Printer, 1787–1825*. Charlottesville, Virginia, 1967.

Snyder, Martin P. *City of Independence: Views of Philadelphia before 1800*. New York, 1975.

——. "William Birch: His Philadelphia Views," *The Pennsylvania Magazine of History and Biography*. Vol. 48 (1949) 271–315.

Stauffer, David McNeely. *American Engravers upon Copper and Steel*, 2 volumes. New York, 1907.

Stokes, I. N. Phelps. *The Iconography of Manhattan Island, 1498–1909*, 6 volumes. New York, 1915–1928.

Stokes, I. N. Phelps, and Daniel C. Haskell. *American Historical Prints: Early Views of American Cities, etc., from the Phelps Stokes and Other Collections*. New York, 1932.

Thompson, Ralph. *American Literary Annuals and Gift Books, 1825–1865*. New York, 1936.

Tyler, Ron, et al. *American Frontier Life: Early Western Painting and Prints*. Fort Worth, Texas, 1987.

Updike, Daniel Berkeley. *Printing Types, Their History, Forms, and Use*. 2 volumes. Cambridge, 1922.

Van Horne, John C. *Pierre Eugene du Simitière*. Philadelphia, 1985.

von Hagen, Victor Wolfgang. *F. Catherwood, Architect-Explorer of Two Worlds*. Barre, Massachusetts, 1968.

——. *Frederick Catherwood, Archt*. New York, 1950.

Wainwright, Nicholas Biddle. "Augustus Köllner, Artist," *The Pennsylvania Magazine of History and Biography*, Vol. 84 (July 1960) 325–351.

——. *One Hundred and Fifty Years of Collecting by the Historical Society of Pennsylvania*, 1824–1974. Philadelphia, 1974.

——. *Philadelphia in the Romantic Age of Lithography*. Philadelphia, 1958.

Ward, Gerald W. R., editor. *The American Illustrated Book in the Nineteenth Century*. Winterthur, Delaware, 1987.

Weitenkampf, Frank. "John Hill and American Landscapes in Aquatint," *American Collector*, Vol. 17 (July 1948) 6–8.

Winterich, John T. *Early American Books and Printing*. Boston and New York, 1935.

Wroth, Lawrence C. *The Colonial Printer*. New York, 1931.

Young, William. *A Dictionary of American Artists, Sculptors, and Engravers*. Cambridge, Massachusetts, 1968.

Index

DESIGNED, PRINTED, AND BOUND
BY MERIDEN-STINEHOUR PRESS
LUNENBURG, VERMONT
PHOTOGRAPHY BY
CLEM FIORI